POEMS, QU

THINGS TO THINK

ABOUT

JIM STOVALL

New York Times Best-Selling Author

Creative Force Press

Creative Force Press

Poems, Quotes, and Things to Think About
© 2014 by Jim Stovall
www.JimStovall.com

This title is also available as an eBook. Visit
www.CreativeForcePress.com/titles for more information.

Published by Creative Force Press
4704 Pacific Ave, Suite C, Lacey, WA 98503
www.CreativeForcePress.com

ISBN: 978-1-939989-13-0

Printed in the United States of America

Dedication

This book is dedicated to

Dorothy Thompson
for taking my words and turning them into books,
and to her mother,
Joye Kanelakos,
for being a hidden treasure
of the written word,
whose work I am proud to include
in this project.

About the Author

Jim Stovall has been a National Olympic weightlifting champion, the President of the Emmy Award-winning Narrative Television Network, and a highly sought-after author and platform speaker. He is the bestselling author of 27 books. Four of his books have been made into movies including *The Ultimate Gift*, which is now a major motion picture starring James Garner and Abigail Breslin.

Steve Forbes, president and CEO of *Forbes* magazine, says, "Jim Stovall is one of the most extraordinary men of our era."

For his work in making television accessible to our nation's 13 million blind and visually impaired people, The President's Committee on Equal Opportunity selected Jim Stovall as the Entrepreneur of the Year. He was also chosen as the International Humanitarian of the Year, joining Jimmy Carter, Nancy Reagan, and Mother Teresa as recipients of this honor.

Jim Stovall can be reached at 918-627-1000.

For more information, please visit
www.JimStovall.com.

INTRODUCTION

When it's all said and done, there's a lot more said than done. Actions always speak louder than words, and talk is cheap. However, words — properly turned — are the source of energy that drives humans to action and ultimately makes the world we live in go around.

All great people throughout history adopted a quote, a phrase, or a personal motto that defined their essence. I hope that somewhere between the covers of this book, you will find a few words that will launch your imagination toward your own destiny.

I have had the privilege of writing a number of books and many newspaper columns. I have had the honor of interviewing some of the greatest human beings of our time. The best of all of these words have been brought together in this volume in hopes that there will be something for everyone.

Success is certainly not a one-size-fits-all proposition. However, somewhere in the world there is a custom-made idea designed just for you. In these pages, my greatest hope is that you and I will find it together.

Jim Stovall, 2014

Poems, Quotes and Things to Think About

I've seen people recover physical abilities, yet never get over emotional trauma after a serious accident. I've seen other people overcome the psychological and emotional trauma of a serious illness, even though they may never regain fully their physical capabilities. Which is the greater healing? Which is the better recovery?

If I had the option of living a mediocre life with eyesight or of living the life I have today, even though I am blind, I'd stay blind and keep the life I have.

> Jim Stovall, as quoted in *Reader's Digest*; June, 1997, from *You Don't Have To Be Blind To See*

Faith is all that dreamers need to see into the future.

> Jim Stovall
> from *The Ultimate Gift*

What is it in our lives we're holding onto that we really don't want or need that is keeping us from total success and our ultimate goal? Failure and success cannot occupy the same space. You must let go of one to begin enjoying the other.

> Jim Stovall
> from *Winners' Wisdom*

9

Only when we rise above our current circumstance and escape from the day-to-day can we really explore the possibilities of our lives.

Douglas Fairbanks, Jr.
from *Success Secrets of Super Achievers*

The next time you find yourself experiencing that life of "quiet desperation," examine your soul and determine what is missing. Therein lies the key to your happiness.

Jim Stovall
from *Wisdom for Winners*

There seems to be a hunger which drives the soul of man. Although the pull is often evasive, directions and choices still beckon, and trails will unwind until we find ourselves traveling in a fluid direction. Our likes, our preferences, our choices have led us as surely as if we had followed a map. Some call it luck, whether good or bad; others call it destination.

Joye Kanelakos
from *The Ultimate Life*

There is nothing more vital than laughter.

Jim Stovall
from *Wisdom of the Ages*

There are a few people who make the right decisions, and there are a few people who make the wrong decisions, but the vast majority of people really never make a decision at all. They simply complain about the results.

> Jim Stovall
> from *Wisdom for Winners*

You are your greatest asset. Invest first and foremost in yourself.

> Jim Stovall
> from *You Don't Have To Be Blind To See*

Remember, you can lose your money and make more, but you can never replace your time.

> Jim Stovall
> from *The Millionaire Map*

Successful people are no different from you and me. In them, you will not see a different species of human being, but you *will* see the same doubts and fears that you face, and you *will* see their greatness and potential in yourself.

> Jim Stovall
> from *Success Secrets of Super Achievers*

Today's defeat is the seed of tomorrow's victory.

Jim Stovall
from *You Don't Have To Be Blind To See*

It is important to realize that in every tragedy and in every problem, there is a potential gift and a seed of greater good. This is what I call the adversity advantage. It is important to remember that the adversity carries no automatic benefit with it, but our reaction to the adversity can make all the difference. For every person you can show me defeated by circumstances, I will show you another individual facing the same circumstances who has turned the adversity into an advantage and moves forward as a better, stronger person with a heightened sense of destiny for their life.

Jim Stovall
from *Wisdom for Winners*

The wisdom of the ages, the answer to any questions, the ability to be informed, entertained, and educated, is as close as your nearest bookstore or library. The greatest men and women of all times are available via books to share with you their greatest secrets.

Jim Stovall
from *Wisdom for Winners*

I have been quoted as calling Jim Stovall one of the greatest men of our era—not solely for the things he has done, but for the fact that Jim Stovall has dissected his own success and put it on display for others to follow through his speeches, newspaper columns, and books.

> Steve Forbes,
> President, CEO, and Editor-in-Chief
> *Forbes Magazine*
> as quoted in *Ultimate Productivity*

Inspiration can be found packaged between the covers of a book, within the verses of a song, or the stanzas of a poem, but it also resides in the whispering wind, a baby's laugh, and the nightly sunset.

> Jim Stovall
> from *Discovering Joye*

Believe. Just believe.

> Jim Stovall
> from *The Lamp* movie

Dreams are doable. They come true when we make them come true.

> Jim Stovall
> from *You Don't Have To Be Blind To See*

Please do not deprive yourself, your family, or the world of your greatness. Mediocrity is the most selfish pursuit of any human being. *Your success* is the greatest gift that you can give to all of humanity.

> Jim Stovall
> from *Success Secrets of Super Achievers*

In the world of motivating yourself and those around you, a few people make things happen, a few more watch things happen, but the great multitude of people are unaware that anything even *is* happening.

> Jim Stovall
> from *Ultimate Productivity*

There is a saying, "It is better to give than to receive." I place my own creed next to that. "There are givers and takers in the world. The takers eat well; the givers sleep well."

I sleep well.

> Monty Hall
> from *Success Secrets of Super Achievers*

Focus is the key to turning energy into productivity. It turns our dreams into goals into reality.

> Jim Stovall
> from *Winners' Wisdom*

The person who really impacts on this world is, as has always been the case, not an institution, not a committee, and not a person who just happens to have a title; rather it is the truly qualitative individual. The qualitative individual *does* matter in this quantitative world of ours, now as ever.

The very nature of humanity and society, regardless of its size or complexity, will always turn on the act of the individual and, therefore, on the quality of the individual.

Supreme Court Justice Sandra Day O'Connor
from *Success Secrets of Super Achievers*

Success needs no explanation, and failure will bear no excuse.

Jim Stovall
from *The Millionaire Map*

Wisdom is eternal, but knowledge changes and expands moment by moment.

Jim Stovall
from *Wisdom of the Ages*

Dedicate yourself to making each day an investment in your future.

Jim Stovall
from *Wisdom for Winners*

There will come a day when people will read your obituary and consider the mark you have made in this world. On that day, it will be too late to make a difference. Make your mark while you can.

Jim Stovall
from *Wisdom for Winners*

It is a wealthy person, indeed, who calculates riches not in gold but in friends.

Jim Stovall
from *The Ultimate Gift*

A recent psychological study revealed that the number one fear that most people have about disease or disability is the fear of going blind. People fear blindness even above dying.

I feared blindness, too. But more than I fear blindness today, I fear not living. I fear not being my best. I fear not maximizing my potential and not doing everything I can do to achieve what I want to achieve, be who I want to be, and have what I want to have. I fear not trying. I fear not hoping.

Being blind isn't the worst thing that can happen to people. Living without hope is the worst thing.

Jim Stovall
from *You Don't Have To Be Blind To See*

If you can't be a leader, be the best follower you can possibly be. When you do your best, you are a success.

> Jim Stovall
> from *Success Secrets of Super Achievers*

Success in life, be it personal or professional, comes from performing at a high level for an extended period of time.

> Jim Stovall
> from *Wisdom for Winners*

The talents we have are immeasurable. The resources and the possibilities for success are as far away as your willingness to pursue and work hard for them.

> Lynn Johnston
> from *Success Secrets of Super Achievers*

Look into the depths of another's soul and listen,

not only with our ears,

but with our hearts and imagination,

and our silent love.

> Joye Kanelakos
> from *The Ultimate Gift*

Acknowledge the source of your motivation, and use it to propel you toward your personal destiny.

Jim Stovall
from *You Don't Have To Be Blind To See*

TRUTH. The only way to go, with anything, especially love. And, there is absolutely no defense against it; it is the purest communication there is.

Shirley Jones
from *Success Secrets of Super Achievers*

Some families are formed by birth, others by legal documents, and still others are formed through love.

Jim Stovall
from *The Ultimate Life*

The strongly motivated person knows that trying is more important than winning. Pursuing one's sense of personal destiny is the very quest of living, and without that pursuit, life has less meaning, less fulfillment, less joy.

Jim Stovall
from *You Don't Have To Be Blind To See*

Dreams are not a product of our imagination, but we are a product of our dreams.

Jim Stovall
from *Discovering Joye*

You don't begin to live until you've lost everything. Heck, I've lost everything three or four times. It's the perfect place to start.

James Garner
from *The Ultimate Gift* movie

Genius is often simply a matter of looking at things a little bit differently than the rest of the world.

Jim Stovall
from *Wisdom for Winners*

When you communicate with mentors, elders, and those with life experience, avoid asking what they think or what they do now. Instead, ask them what they thought and what they did when they were starting their journey. Encourage them to share their mistakes and the pitfalls they experienced.

Jim Stovall
from *Discovering Joye*

You can have everything you need and even everything you want, but you can't always have *more* for its own sake. *More* doesn't exist. It is a direction but not a destination.

> Jim Stovall
> from *The Millionaire Map*

Mentors lead you by their example and nudge you to become all you can be.

> Jim Stovall
> from *You Don't Have To Be Blind To See*

The ultimate life is nothing more than a series of ultimate days. Today's the day!

> Jim Stovall
> from *The Ultimate Life*

Whatever you do, make a difference. Practice rather than preach. Make of your life an affirmation, defined by your ideals, not the negation of others. Dare to the level of your capability, then go beyond to a higher level. If you would be fit to command men, obey God.

> Alexander Haig
> from *Success Secrets of Super Achievers*

Laughter is a gift the world sorely needs and a legacy we must pass on.

> Jim Stovall
> from *The Gift of a Legacy*

Failure feels the fear and retreats. Success feels the fear and moves forward anyway.

> Jim Stovall
> from *The Way I See The World*

Our family is involved in our life's journey long before we are born and long after we die. Some of our family is connected by blood and others only by love.

> Jim Stovall
> from *The Ultimate Journey*

I discovered that there's a second kind of blindness that everybody has, and it has nothing to do with physical eyes. It has to do with your ability to make sense of your life and then to make the most of your life. It has to do with your true potential — the full scope of your ability as a person to feel, respond, and transform your life and, ultimately, to become the person you were truly created to be.

I may have lost my sight, but in the aftermath, I gained

a greater vision than I had ever had before.

Do you have a vision for your life? You don't have to be blind to see!

Jim Stovall
from *You Don't Have To Be Blind To See*

If I were king, I would average out our allotment of wisdom over the years of our lives. We would have more wisdom when we're younger, when we really need it. We would have newer schools and older jails. Policemen, fire fighters, and teachers would be paid what they deserve. Everyone would be in the same time zone. Wars would be fought by the people who start them. Everyone would be required to work at something they enjoy. Elderly people would be highly sought-after for their wisdom and experience. And every man, woman, or child would know that they were a unique and special gift. Everyone would be allowed to pursue their passion and maximize their talent. But, since the odds are not great of my becoming King of the World, let's all do the best that we can.

Jim Stovall
from *Winners' Wisdom*

Don't let your sense of worth be tied to your finances. You are worth vastly more than that.

Jim Stovall
from *You Don't Have To Be Blind To See*

Success is not a profession; it's the way we approach life.

Jim Stovall
from *Success Secrets of Super Achievers*

I don't really think about the past. What matters is the present. And a huge interest in the future.

Max Schmeling
from *Success Secrets of Super Achievers*

Winners believe that success exists for everyone, and that their success does not diminish anyone else's. Success, they believe, is available in an unlimited supply, like oxygen. They don't hesitate to breathe in all they want or need because for them, it's the natural thing to do. They assume that everyone will breathe in all the oxygen—or in this case, success—that they want, and that it in no way will diminish the infinite supply.

Jim Stovall
from *Success Secrets of Super Achievers*

Life is life. Far more important than what happens to us is what we do in the wake of the experiences.

> Jim Stovall
> from *You Don't Have To Be Blind To See*

Our lives are lived a day at a time, and our legacy is made up of these days.

> Jim Stovall
> from *The Gift of a Legacy*

Your future, along with your personal and professional goals, are not as fragile as you might think. Failure is often the fertilizer that makes future success blossom.

> Jim Stovall
> from *Winners' Wisdom*

Life is ever-changing, and so must we be willing to change to fully appreciate and enjoy all of life's opportunities and adventures.

> Jane Powell
> from *Success Secrets of Super Achievers*

There is a seed of greater good inside you.

> Dr. Harold Paul
> from *You Don't Have To Be Blind To See*

I don't believe you have to be better than everybody else. I believe you have to be better than you ever thought you could be.

Ken Venturi
from *Success Secrets of Super Achievers*

Everybody is blind in some way. Each one of us has blind spots—things we don't see, or don't see accurately, about ourselves, about others, about life as a whole. You may have the full capacity of physical vision, but that doesn't mean you always perceive what lies before you or perceive what is useful, appropriate, accurate, or worthy. Even if you have the capacity for *looking*, you may not have the capability of *seeing*.

There's a big difference. One involves a physical ability. The other requires inner vision and creativity. I wasn't always blind, but I didn't always see.

Jim Stovall
from *You Don't Have To Be Blind To See*

Our future can only be significant if we build it on top of the meaningful tasks that we perform today. Remember that this moment of this day is all we really have.

Jim Stovall
from *Wisdom for Winners*

When faced with a dilemma, I can assure you that the right answer is always to try one more time, because when it comes to your dreams, your goals, and your destiny, it is always too soon to quit.

Jim Stovall
from *The Way I See The World*

Celebrate your family, not in spite of their imperfections but because of them. If families were perfect, they could never include people like you and me.

Jim Stovall
from *Discovering Joye*

Gratitude is a habit that must be developed. It is a muscle that must be exercised regularly.

Jim Stovall
from *Discovering Joye*

You have the power to change your life, but first you must make a conscious and quality decision to find and utilize your unique strengths and talents on your way to your own personal success.

Jim Stovall
from *Ultimate Productivity*

The nature of the work is not as important as the nature of the person. Anyone can learn the steps in doing a job, but only a few people understand the pride, the dignity, and the honor that goes with doing a job well.

Jim Stovall
from *The Ultimate Life*

If you say somebody ought to do something about a particular situation, sit up and take notice. *You* are very likely the *somebody* who should do it.

Jim Stovall
from *You Don't Have To Be Blind To See*

Are you blaming somebody else for your lot in life? Very likely, the reality is that you're blaming the wrong person. Look in the mirror. Some people make right choices and decisions. A few people make wrong choices and decisions. But I've concluded that most people don't know they have a choice.

You have the right to choose! Don't give it away to anybody else.

Jim Stovall
from *You Don't Have To Be Blind To See*

Learning is a journey that never ends. Each discovery reveals another mystery waiting to be understood.

Jim Stovall
from *The Ultimate Journey*

Greatness comes not from being ten times better than anyone else, or even twice as good. It comes when we are willing to invest just a little more of ourselves toward the task at hand. The next time you are faced with a difficult challenge in your life, try viewing it as a turning point that can put you on the path toward the greatness for which you have been destined.

Jim Stovall
from *Winners' Wisdom*

Regardless of your profession or business, you can find a way to use your skills and talents, combined with your money, to make a difference in the world.

Jim Stovall
from *The Millionaire Map*

In the final analysis, time is all we have.

Jim Stovall
from *Wisdom for Winners*

Money can help you do whatever you dream of doing or achieve whatever you desire to have. Use money. But pursue destiny.

Jim Stovall
from *You Don't Have To Be Blind To See*

If you don't choose what you do with your time, somebody else will.

Jim Stovall
from *You Don't Have To Be Blind To See*

Dreams want to come true. So dream the dream, and go for it.

Sheb Wooley
from *Success Secrets of Super Achievers*

Stay fixed on your focal point. Become the most productive person you know, not just the busiest! If you have been productive, you'll be closer to your goal. If you have been busy, you'll just be tired.

Jim Stovall
from *You Don't Have To Be Blind To See*

Anyone attempting to be great at everything is destined, at best, to be average at a lot of things and great at nothing. Move toward your area of greatness.

> Jim Stovall
> from *Wisdom for Winners*

Successful people overcome fears and do what they set out to do, no matter how scared they may be while doing it.

> Jim Stovall
> from *You Don't Have To Be Blind To See*

A journey may be long or short, but it must start at the very spot one finds oneself.

> Jim Stovall
> from *The Ultimate Gift*

When I was very young, our family was very poor and I was very sorry for myself. Then I observed that almost everyone had problems — financial, physical, racial — all kinds of problems. I decided that the only thing that defeats people is accepting defeat.

> Mort Walker
> from *Success Secrets of Super Achievers*

Pursue your dreams as if you will live forever, and consider your legacy as if this were your final day.

Jim Stovall
from *Wisdom for Winners*

We have life as long as our heart is beating, but we live as long as our heart is filled.

Jim Stovall
from *The Gift of a Legacy*

The first step you make toward the realization of your dream may be a very small one. It may seem insignificant to others and even to you. But the first step is always the first step. And that makes it important, no matter how small it is.

Jim Stovall
from *You Don't Have To Be Blind To See*

You must take ownership of your life. It's *your* life. You are where you are because of decisions you have made in the past, and if you don't like the life you're living, you can do something to change it.

Jim Stovall
from *You Don't Have To Be Blind To See*

SOMEONE GREATER THAN I

Someone greater than I

Put this dream in my soul.

Someone greater than I

Has His hand in it all.

The dream is coming together

Because of someone much greater.

Someone greater than I

Is in control.

Music and lyrics by Kelly Morrison

Sight does not happen in the eye, even as hearing does not happen in the ear. Sighted persons do not "see" many things in front of them. They only "see" what they are focused on, thinking about, aware of in their mind and spirit.

So the person who is really blind is the person who is distracted from reality by anxieties or fears or other negative thoughts.

Dr. Robert Schuller
from *Success Secrets of Super Achievers*

There's a seed of life in every dream or goal that a person sets for himself.

> Jim Stovall
> from *You Don't Have To Be Blind To See*

If you believe that millionaires are different from you, your life will be filled with financial starvation while everyone around you enjoys an economic banquet.

> Jim Stovall
> from *The Millionaire Map*

I wonder if my life had been
Of some completely different vein
Would I have scaled more lofty heights,
Waved more banners, flashed more lights,
And pressed my head where royalty has lain?

Or what if I asked but to see
Exquisite beauty, just for me?
Would I have ever dared to look
Beyond the diary or the book
That held the secrets wise men left
For such as we, for such as we?

Joye Kanelakos
from *The Ultimate Journey* and *Discovering Joye*

Ask yourself: Why am I doing what I'm doing in life? If the answer to that question doesn't motivate you and those around you, find something else to do—and *quick*.

> Jim Stovall
> from *Ultimate Productivity*

Every day dawns filled with promise, potential, and possibility.

> Jim Stovall
> from *The Lamp*

The first time I stepped out of my house as a blind person and walked to my mailbox I was barely moving and scared stiff. The five hundredth time I stepped out of my house and walked the length of my driveway, I didn't even think about being nervous. I just went to the mailbox and came back to the house.

I could just as easily have stumbled on the five hundredth trip as I could have on the first, but by the time I'd made five hundred trips, I also knew that if I tripped over something, I could get up, dust myself off, and still get myself to the end of the driveway and back to the house.

Nothing about the driveway or the potential hazards had changed. *I* had changed. And that's the way it is with any success.

The problems and obstacles and challenges may not be any different. They may be bigger. But you and your ability to take on that challenge have grown even greater proportionally. You are better able to take the next step, and in that lies all the difference in the world.

Jim Stovall
from *You Don't Have To Be Blind To See*

Struggles often serve to release the wisdom, patience, and strength we all possess but too seldom demonstrate. Rarely are people at their best when circumstances are good, but when tragedy strikes or obstacles appear, you will find superhuman traits being displayed.

Jim Stovall
from *Wisdom for Winners*

You don't have to be light-years better than anybody else to be successful. Comparison isn't a part of the process. You simply need to pursue the goal within yourself of being a little bit better tomorrow than you are today.

Jim Stovall
from *You Don't Have To Be Blind To See*

Because parents mold and shape who we are as individuals, they ultimately determine what we become as a people.

Jim Stovall
from *Wisdom of the Ages*

Everyone has problems! It is part of our mortal experience. We have troubles to teach us patience, humility, and long-suffering, and most important, to bring us closer to our faith. However, it is not the problems that count but the manner in which we handle them. Our attitude is one of the most important fundamental aspects of our lives.

Gary Player
from *Success Secrets of Super Achievers*

Knowledge is the key to wealth.

Jim Stovall
from *Wisdom for Winners*

One of the traits that great and famous people have in common is a sense of expectation and destiny. They always believed that they were destined for greatness.

Jim Stovall
from *Success Secrets of Super Achievers*

As we journey into our future, we begin to understand our past in ways that help us travel today.

> Jim Stovall
> from *The Ultimate Journey*

Everything worthwhile, everything of any value, has a price. The price is effort.

> Loretta Young
> from *Success Secrets of Super Achievers*

Education is a lifelong journey whose destination expands as you travel.

> Jim Stovall
> from *The Ultimate Gift*

Always remember this: A big dream doesn't cost any more than a little one.

> Jim Stovall
> from *You Don't Have To Be Blind To See*

You get what you expect, and I'm here to tell you that you can expect more.

> Jim Stovall
> from *You Don't Have To Be Blind To See*

The mistakes you make as you pursue your goal are examples of what doesn't work. They aren't failures. They're points of learning!

> Jim Stovall
> from *You Don't Have To Be Blind To See*

Family is a legacy we receive and one we pass along. Some of our family members are connected by blood — others through love.

> Jim Stovall
> from *The Gift of a Legacy*

You change your life when you change your mind.

> Jim Stovall
> from *Wisdom for Winners*

Success is a state of mind. The personal triumphs that one achieves as a result of his or her own efforts are many times more valuable than the accidental attainment of any prize. Success, to me, means winning my own approval...and happiness goes hand in hand with success.

> Robert Shapiro
> from *Success Secrets of Super Achievers*

Becoming a millionaire is not about convincing everyone else that you are a millionaire. It does not involve any specific possessions or number of zeroes on a bank or brokerage account. Becoming a millionaire is, first and foremost, a matter of living your life on your own terms.

Jim Stovall
from *The Millionaire Map*

Don't ever confuse activity with productivity, and remember that speed is not necessarily progress.

Jim Stovall
from *Wisdom for Winners*

Sometimes you do the right thing and it makes a difference...not only at that moment in time, but for generations to come.

Eddie Albert
from *Success Secrets of Super Achievers*

Focus on the important things in your day, and take every opportunity you can to go fishing.

Jim Stovall
from *Wisdom for Winners*

Someone asked Conrad Hilton when he knew he was successful. He said that he knew he was successful while he was still sleeping on a park bench because he knew that once he had made his mind up to become successful, he had taken the first step on his journey to success.

> Jim Stovall
> from *You Don't Have To Be Blind To See*

Choice requires personal courage. Don't be afraid to lasso a dream.

> Jim Stovall
> from *You Don't Have To Be Blind To See*

To achieve balance doesn't mean to bring every element of your life to a level of mediocrity. It means to raise every element to excellence.

> Jim Stovall
> from *You Don't Have To Be Blind To See*

The more we care for the happiness of others, the greater is our own sense of well-being. It is the ultimate source of happiness in life.

> His Holiness the Dalai Lama
> from *Success Secrets of Super Achievers*

In this life, work is the culmination of all we are and all we learn that we bring to others through the marketplace.

> Jim Stovall
> from *The Ultimate Life*

Good-natured friends are the richness of old age.

> Joye Kanelakos
> from *Discovering Joye*

If you are not where you want to be along the road to success, you may want to examine not only how hard you are working, but what you are working on.

> Jim Stovall
> from *Wisdom for Winners*

Set the highest hurdles up *first*. Once you clear them, it's downhill for the rest of the day.

> Jim Stovall
> from *Ultimate Productivity*

Any time a giver and a receiver come together, they both depart richer, better, wiser, and filled with gratitude.

> Jim Stovall
> from *Discovering Joye*

If we are not allowed to deal with small problems, we will be destroyed by slightly larger ones. When we come to understand this fact, we live our lives not avoiding problems but welcoming them as challenges that will strengthen us so that we can be victorious in the future.

Jim Stovall
from *The Ultimate Life*

Discover the library. Books can change your life. The greatest leaders of all time are waiting to share their secrets and wisdom if you will but take the time to listen.

Jim Stovall
from *Success Secrets of Super Achievers*

Good health is its own reward.

Jim Stovall
from *Wisdom of the Ages*

Remember that yesterday is history, tomorrow is a mystery, and today is a gift. That's why it's called "the present." Be sure to live it that way and plan to live it that way in the future.

Jim Stovall
from *Wisdom for Winners*

Success is never a one-size-fits-all proposition. It is a custom-tailored, one-of-a-kind suit, lovingly made with no one in mind other than you.

Jim Stovall
from *Ultimate Productivity*

If you have any leadership role whatsoever, take heed. You are being watched, and what you do will influence others whether you like it or not. You owe the people who are watching you your best effort — to be, do, and have the very highest quality in your life.

Jim Stovall
from *You Don't Have To Be Blind To See*

There is no such thing as a money shortage. There is plenty of money in this world. What we have is a motivation, creativity, or idea shortage.

Jim Stovall
from *You Don't Have To Be Blind To See*

People find gold in fields, veins, riverbeds, and pockets. But wherever you find gold, it takes work to get it out.

Art Linkletter
from *Success Secrets of Super Achievers*

ONE LIFE

Only one life.

One life to live.

What will you do with it?

Only one life.

One life to give.

What will you do with it?

Treat it like a treasure,

Like an hour glass,

And the sand slips away.

Set aside your worries.

Take away the hurries.

Don't miss your chance to live.

Live today.

Music and lyrics by Kelly Morrison
from the motion picture *The Ultimate Life*

We do not always get what we want or deserve or earn, but we do inevitably get what we expect. We move inexorably toward our most dominant thought, so we always find what we're looking for. If you set out today thinking that this is going to be a bad day, shortly things will begin to order themselves to meet your expectation. Conversely, if you set out with an expectation of greatness, this can be one of the greatest days of your life.

Please do me a favor. For one day, expect great things to happen; look for them at every turn; and watch them come to pass. By the time you put your head on your pillow, you will have enjoyed an exceptional day.

Jim Stovall
From *Winners' Wisdom*

The ability to understand and be understood is at the heart of all agreements and human interaction.

Jim Stovall
from *Wisdom of the Ages*

If you don't know where you're going how will you ever know when you get there? People who don't make a choice are no better off than people who don't have a choice.

Jim Stovall
from *Wisdom for Winners*

Don't strive for money, wealth, power, and fame. It will come naturally when you follow your passion.

Barry Newman
from *Success Secrets of Super Achievers*

If you have a life's goal or what you consider to be your destiny, you should be taking some action on it every day. There is always something to learn, someone to meet, or some preparation you can take toward that end. Dedicate yourself to making each day an investment in your future.

> Jim Stovall
> from *Wisdom for Winners*

Money is nothing more than a tool. It can be a force for good, a force for evil, or simply be idle.

> Jim Stovall
> from *The Ultimate Gift*

Greatness isn't something you acquire. It's something you choose to be. It's a quality of the heart and soul.

> Jim Stovall
> from *You Don't Have To Be Blind To See*

Explore not only the "great lives of great people" but also great lives being lived by ordinary people who have great goals, vision, or passion.

> Jim Stovall
> from *Success Secrets of Super Achievers*

Money is a tool that can be used in virtually any way we choose. More than anything else, money represents choices. Money can buy the most useful and beneficial things in the world, or it can purchase frustration and destruction.

Jim Stovall
from *The Millionaire Map*

People spend more time planning their three-day weekend than they do planning how they are going to live the rest of their lives.

Jim Stovall
from *Wisdom for Winners*

A journey of a thousand miles is nothing more than a series of single steps, but if you stop or take a detour on any one of those steps, you will not reach your destination.

Jim Stovall
from *Ultimate Productivity*

None of us does anything we don't get paid for. If we're lazy and do nothing, we likely get nothing. Our reward is linked to our effort.

But if you invest effort in furthering your dreams and goals in life, you *always* get paid. That's a principle of life. If nothing more, your expenditure of time, energy, and talent will have made you into a different person. It will have altered you in some way. And as your identity changes, things around you will change. The reward may not be in tangible things, but may lie in what happens inside you — and therefore, what is capable of flowing out of you to others. Either way, you are rewarded.

Jim Stovall
from *You Don't Have To Be Blind To See*

When we do not have firmly established priorities, we are controlled by people who do.

Jim Stovall
from *Wisdom for Winners*

Learning is a lifelong, never-ending pursuit. The great paradox exists that the more you know, the more you realize you don't know.

Jim Stovall
from *Discovering Joye*

We will leave many legacies behind. Money is an important tool but the least valuable of all our legacies.

Jim Stovall
from *The Gift of a Legacy*

Relationships are the spice of life. People we love magnify our emotions and multiply our love many times over. The best single thing that you can do immediately to improve your relationship is to improve yourself.

Jim Stovall
from *The Way I See the World*

Time is the only commodity you truly have.

Jim Stovall
from *You Don't Have To Be Blind To See*

He who loves his work never labors.

Jim Stovall
from *The Ultimate Gift*

The things we learn are a legacy we receive. The things we teach are a legacy we leave behind.

Jim Stovall
from *The Gift of a Legacy*

For everyone who turns a disadvantage into an excuse, there is someone else who turns it into a springboard to greatness.

Jim Stovall
from *Wisdom for Winners*

True wisdom speaks to the common needs of all people.

Jim Stovall
from *Wisdom of the Ages*

So many of us suffer from the success/achievement/rat-race syndrome which says you matter only because you have made it. Most of us think that this attitude carries over into our relationship with God; that God loves us because we are lovable, we deserve to be loved, and we have made it by impressing God. The truth is that God loves me. Period. That is the most fundamental truth about you, about me. It is a free gift, unearned, undeserved.

God loves me not because I am lovable. I am lovable because God loves me. That is what gives me my worth and nothing can change it.

The Most Reverend Desmond M. Tutu
from *Success Secrets of Super Achievers*

You won't succeed because you're better than anyone else. You'll succeed because success has been defined by *you*, and there is no one more ready, willing, or able to fill your unique role than *you*.

Jim Stovall
from *Ultimate Productivity*

January, 1989

The world awaits as morning breaks
Above the rim of a shimmering hill;
Color showers the skies awake
And the trees stand breathless and still.

Silence reigns with a gentle hand
As life, still cradled in its hold,
Stretches to greet the waking land
All sprinkled now with silver and gold.

Joye Kanelakos
from *Discovering Joye*

No journey worth taking ever begins or ends alone. It always includes the people we care about.

Jim Stovall
from *The Millionaire Map*

Nobody is born with a good attitude or a bad attitude. You allow yourself to respond to life's circumstances in particular ways. Stay positive. Even if you fail, look for the lesson learned and apply it to your life.

Jim Stovall
from *You Don't Have To Be Blind To See*

Success is a destination while your mission is that ongoing, constant journey toward success.

Jim Stovall
from *Ultimate Productivity*

Invest your days in the pursuit of a worthwhile summit, but enjoy each day of the climb.

Jim Stovall
from *Wisdom for Winners*

Once you have arrived at a place in your life that is satisfying and safe, it is tempting to stay right there. But if your dream is a little bigger than the opportunities being offered, sometimes you have to get out of the boat and swim for a distant shore.

Jim Stovall
from *Success Secrets of Super Achievers*

A journey should never be judged by the destination or mode of transportation. It should be judged by the friends who accompany us on the trip.

Jim Stovall
from *The Ultimate Journey*

Visualization is mental rehearsal.

> Jim Stovall
> from *You Don't Have To Be Blind To See*

One must invest work and energy for the expectation of reward in the future.

> Jim Stovall
> from *Wisdom of the Ages*

Golf was not Ken Venturi's first career choice. He thought he would become a dentist and play golf for fun. Instead, he turned pro in 1956 and proceeded to have four outstanding years. In 1961, however, he hit a slump that made him the invisible man in professional golf.

Then came 1964. Suffering from heat exhaustion, he nonetheless managed to win the U.S. Open. For this inspiring feat, he was named "Sportsman of the Year" by *Sports Illustrated*, and PGA Player of the Year. End of story? Not hardly. Shortly after his dramatic victory, he developed a rare circulatory and nerve ailment in his hands that forced him into surgery and therapy. Determination brought him back to the tour, where he regained his style and continued to play golf for the rest of his career.

His new career, commentating, seems like a natural

choice...unless you know that he had to overcome stuttering to make the grade. So, you see, some successes are hard-won.

Jim Stovall
from *Success Secrets of Super Achievers*

Refuse to blink. Stare down the big lies!

Lie #1: I can't have a great destiny.

Lie #2: I shouldn't be, do, or have what I am dreaming about as my personal destiny and goal of success.

Lie #3: I can try, but I won't make it.

Lie #4: I really don't want that.

Jim Stovall
from *You Don't Have To Be Blind To See*

Very few people would say that their happiest moments were when they made their most money, but rather, when they felt the real possibility of achieving their dream.

I was told, and I believe, that a person needs three things to be happy: someone to love, something to do, and something to look forward to.

Happiness is just that simple. Success is simply icing on the cake.

Kenny Rogers
from *Success Secrets of Super Achievers*

If you don't know what you're doing in the world, how will you ever know what in the world you are doing?

> Jim Stovall
> from *Wisdom for Winners*

Your past has defined who you are today. The action you take today will define who you will be in the future, unless you fail to release your past.

> Jim Stovall
> from *Ultimate Productivity*

In the Chinese language, symbols are used to express thoughts and ideas, and not just individual words. The symbol for *crisis* has long been identified with the ancient Chinese mariners who viewed *crisis* as "opportunity on a dangerous wind." The same stormy seas that threaten to founder our ship can often propel us toward a Promised Land that we never before imagined.

> Jim Stovall
> from *Winners' Wisdom*

Life's journey is often along a rough and rocky uphill road. Laughter can lighten the load.

> Jim Stovall
> from *The Ultimate Journey*

While we are grateful for the legacies others have left us, the only tribute we can give to those who have gone before is to leave our own legacy.

Jim Stovall
from *The Gift of a Legacy*

When it comes to achieving your millionaire status, or any other significant goal in your life, the first and only person you need to impress is yourself.

Jim Stovall
from *The Millionaire Map*

There he was, standing by my hospital room door, bracing his small body on a single crutch. A blue-eyed, tousled-blond-haired, midsized, handsome boy of ten or so with a soft southern accent and an easy, quick smile. He had heard from the nurses down in pediatrics that I was in the hospital, with hepatitis. Whether he knew who I was, I'm not sure, but I was a sick puppy in a downward spiral of depression.

He had a picture just for me that he had painted. It was a wonderful watercolor. Bright and happy, the scene was of his home, and he was hoping the picture would cheer me up. It did, but not just for the artistry or for the caring his good heart was sharing.

It was in the picture, itself, that I realized the strength and courage of the young man before me. Through this act, he made me stop feeling sorry for myself, and I started to improve.

I've saved that picture he painted, and as always I draw strength from his little self-portrait down in the corner: a blue-eyed, tousled-blonde-haired young boy with just one leg.

Lee Meriwether
from *Success Secrets of Super Achievers*

This world is a stage

And this life a performance.

We all are players

Waiting for our moment in the sun.

We strive to please

The crowd before us

'Til we learn

Our true audience

Is a crowd

Of only one.

Jim Stovall

The view we have into the future is only possible because we are standing on the shoulders of the giants who have gone before us. Their lives and words teach us lessons. If we learn from these lessons, the future will be brighter than ever. If we do not learn from these lessons, we will be forced to repeat the struggles of the past.

> Jim Stovall
> from *Wisdom for Winners*

It might be tempting at times to use a challenge as an excuse for not succeeding, but it is smarter to go around, over, under, or through the obstacle so that you can take advantage of the good things waiting for you on the other side.

> Jim Stovall
> from *Success Secrets of Super Achievers*

I heard an inspiring story recently about the associate choreographer for the Miss America Pageant.

After he had auditioned for the job by dancing—and had been selected—he went to see the director of choreography. "I have to tell you something," he said. "Don't worry," she said, "you have the job." But he insisted, "I have to tell you that I was born without legs." The director gasped in disbelief, and when she had composed herself, she asked,

"If you were born without legs, then why in the world did you decide to become a dancer?

"Because," he said, "it was the one thing they said I could never do."

Always remember this: It's never easy.

Richard Valeriani
from *Success Secrets of Super Achievers*

Strive to have extraordinary days while living in a normal world. It doesn't take much to elevate yourself above the crowd.

Jim Stovall
from *Wisdom for Winners*

The number one motivational voice to which you will respond is your own voice.

Jim Stovall
from *You Don't Have To Be Blind To See*

Regardless of age, at daybreak there is a newness, a beginning again when everything starts afresh and the comforting promises of God may once again be heard in every quieted heart.

Joye Kanelakos, from her personal diary

The journey of life is a gift we have been given. Our lives should be lived as gifts to those who follow.

> Jim Stovall
> from *The Ultimate Journey*

Never pass along your valuables unless you have passed along your values.

> Jim Stovall
> from *The Millionaire Map*

Our families are the measuring stick by which we judge the rest of the world.

> Jim Stovall
> from *Discovering Joye*

Never seek an opinion or accept criticism from someone who does not have what you want. Seek out the counsel of mentors and peers who are achievers. Seek their counsel, accept their criticism, and utilize their performance as a measuring stick for your own.

> Jim Stovall
> from *Wisdom for Winners*

Associate with other people of destiny.

>Jim Stovall
>from *You Don't Have To Be Blind To See*

My wish for you is that all your dreams will come true, and as you stand atop the mountain, having reached each of your goals, you will accept that as an opportunity to dream bigger dreams, set greater goals, and leave a lasting legacy for those who will travel behind you.

>Jim Stovall
>from *The Gift of a Legacy*

The first step is the most difficult. The second step is the next most difficult, but the more steps you take toward the total fulfillment of a dream, the faster those steps seem to fall into line, and the easier it is to take the next step that presents itself.

>Jim Stovall
>from *You Don't Have To Be Blind To See*

Not all poetry contains wisdom, but at the heart of all wisdom, one will find poetry.

>Jim Stovall
>from *Wisdom of the Ages*

I think success and happiness go together—if you do what makes you happy, you'll most likely be successful.

(Of course, you shouldn't do just *anything* that makes you happy; here, I'm thinking of the Unabomber.)

Dave Barry
from *Success Secrets of Super Achievers*

Success is vitally important but virtually impossible to define. Success is not a direction, a speed, or an amount. It is, instead, the fulfillment of our deepest desires and greatest potential. You and I must take on our own quest for success as a personal proposition that only we can define and only we can create.

Jim Stovall
from *Wisdom for Winners*

The only thing I have learned about success is that if one is willing to listen, *really* listen, to things that are said, as well as to things that are *not* said, that person will be miles ahead of the competition. Those who have never learned to listen, never truly understand the human heart.

Joseph Wambaugh
from *Success Secrets of Super Achievers*

You can become the greatest financial success the world has ever known, but if you lose your family and ruin your health in the process, you will not be successful.

Jim Stovall
from *Ultimate Productivity*

We must all find a way to make our career a pursuit of our passion and a means to our lasting legacy.

Jim Stovall
from *Discovering Joye*

Dreams and goals develop over time. The more you give wings to a dream, the greater the possibility that dream will move in a direction you hadn't anticipated. Dreams rarely stay fixed very long. Dreams flow from our creativity, and because they do, they change with the flow of our lives. They are like water moving over hard ground — they form channels and rivulets and take on direction.

Don't pounce on a dream or goal too quickly. Give it time to sink deep within your being. When you find the dream or goal that recurs, go with it.

Jim Stovall
from *You Don't Have To Be Blind To See*

As you reach your millionaire destination, you should help others along their route and leave a legacy for future travelers.

> Jim Stovall
> from *The Millionaire Map*

When we learn, knowledge has been imparted. When we teach others, it has been transferred. But, the magic of mentoring happens when we teach others to teach. Then and only then does the knowledge become the property of everyone who can benefit from learning, teaching, and sharing.

> Jim Stovall
> from *Winners' Wisdom*

Opportunity abounds. All of the best ideas haven't been thought. All of the money in the world is not in somebody else's bank account.

> Jim Stovall
> from *You Don't Have To Be Blind To See*

Successful people follow through. They demand excellence at the detail level.

> Jim Stovall
> from *You Don't Have To Be Blind To See*

The single characteristic shared by more top executives is the fact that they read or listen to positive, motivational, affirming material on a regular basis.

Jim Stovall
from *Wisdom for Winners*

SEASONS OF CHANGE

Like a rose that has its glory time to shine
People know that it will find its time to die.
Like a tree that flaunts its leaves in summer's breeze,
The snow will surely come to change the summer scene.

Like the riches that become man's closest friend,
They come from dust and to the dust they'll go again.
Like the joy that comes from loving with the heart,
Turns to sorrow when a loved one has to part.

There's a time for laughter,
There's a time for pain,
There's a time for glory,
There's a time for rain.
There is a God whose love remains
Every time the seasons change.

Kelly Morrison,
from the album *Seasons of Change,* by Kelly Morrison

Everyone strives to reach a state of "normality." This process of normalizing everyone is akin to seeking the lowest common human denominator. This is to say, if you never stand out you will certainly never be outstanding.

You will find that the real achievers in this world rarely do anything "normally." Monuments are never erected to "normal" people. They are erected to people dedicated to doing one thing exceedingly well. Find that thing in your life, and avoid the temptation to be "normal."

Jim Stovall
from *Winners' Wisdom*

If you divide all the money in the world evenly, very shortly, the millionaires will emerge again.

Jim Stovall
from *Wisdom for Winners*

As someone who lost both of my parents in a concentration camp and grew up as an exiled prisoner myself, I think I understand the power and the value of a free society as well as anyone. The freedoms we have make everything possible.

Dr. Ruth Westheimer
from *Success Secrets of Super Achievers*

Humanity develops and expands from the power of collective knowledge.

Jim Stovall
from *Wisdom of the Ages*

They say that wisdom comes with age, but they don't say you can't cut a few corners and learn from someone else's experience.

Jim Stovall
from *Success Secrets of Super Achievers*

Often, the greatest gifts are ones that cost very little or nothing at all. When it's all said and done, the best gift any of us have is the gift of this day and how we share it.

Jim Stovall
from *Wisdom for Winners*

A sense of urgency is the most vital element in your success. There are many great ideas that never amount to anything more than a great idea because we fail to take that all-important first step.

Jim Stovall
from *Winners' Wisdom*

More people fail, not because they are unable to reach their goals, but because they have wrongly defined both their goals and the meaning of success.

Jim Stovall
from *Ultimate Productivity*

We are only as big as the smallest thing it takes to divert us from our goals and dreams.

Jim Stovall
from *Wisdom for Winners*

In the end, a person is only known by the impact he has on others.

Jim Stovall
from *The Ultimate Gift*

Success demands that you get out of your comfort zone and take a risk. Success begins by feeling uncomfortable.

Jim Stovall
from *You Don't Have To Be Blind To See*

The meaning of life is to find out gift, and the purpose of life is to give it away.

Jim Stovall
from *Discovering Joye*

Make a list of the things that have to be done today in order to get one step closer to your personal definition of success.

Jim Stovall
from *Ultimate Productivity*

Problems viewed in the future appear to be obstacles while problems viewed in the past are revealed as blessings.

Jim Stovall
from *The Ultimate Life*

After 75 years as an occupant of this planet Earth, I have only this to say: Life is the most precious gift ever given.

It knows not of good or ill. If we treat it with love and respect, in ourselves and in others, it will return to us fulfillment.

James Whitmore
from *Success Secrets of Super Achievers*

Money is nothing more or less than a result of creating value in the lives of other people.

Jim Stovall
from *Wisdom for Winners*

The wonders of the modern world around us are the legacy that dreamers who have gone before bequeathed to us.

> Jim Stovall
> from *The Gift of a Legacy*

In this life, the most average day can take an extraordinary turn; therefore, each day should be anticipated and savored as a gift.

> Jim Stovall
> from *The Ultimate Life*

Succinctly put, our three keys to success are PREPARATION, PREPARATION, and PREPARATION. Always remain focused, and never let anyone deter you from achieving your dreams.

> Johnnie Cochran, Jr.
> from *Success Secrets of Super Achievers*

You may not be able to embrace the concept of a great, fabulous, wonderful success in your life. But will you at least accept this possibility, "Maybe — just *maybe* — there's a chance you can have a better tomorrow. Maybe — just *maybe* — there's a shot you can take, a decision you can make, an option you can exercise, a choice you can act on that will make a difference. Maybe—just *maybe*—tomorrow can be better than today"?

Starting now.

Jim Stovall
from *You Don't Have To Be Blind To See*

The proverbial headlong quest to keep up with the Joneses has kept many people from becoming truly wealthy.

Jim Stovall
from *The Millionaire Map*

Heroes are not extraordinary people. They are ordinary people who conduct themselves in extraordinary ways.

Jim Stovall
from *Winners' Wisdom*

Friendship should be measured by dependability in times of difficulty.

Jim Stovall
from *Wisdom for Winners*

Sharpen your mind's eye. To claim the gold medal of your destiny, you first must see it.

Jim Stovall
from *You Don't Have To Be Blind To See*

Once you've taken a positive step forward, you are out of a failure mode and into a remedy mode. And, once you start thinking about remedies, you begin to think in practical, concrete terms that will point you toward a direction. Once you have a direction to go, *GO!*

Jim Stovall
from *You Don't Have To Be Blind To See*

When I was playing baseball in California for the Dodgers, one of the studios called the team and asked about putting me in a small part. I was sure they wanted me to play a ballplayer. The next day, I showed up at the studio. Not only did they *not* want me to be a ballplayer, in my first scene I was teamed up with Katharine Hepburn and Spencer Tracy!

I remember asking Spencer how you do this, and he said that the key to acting is to "show up on time, know your lines, and hit your mark. And, never forget to have fun."

It took me a long time to get the first three, but from the first day on, I have always had fun. And, having fun is the key to *everything*.

Chuck Connors
from *Success Secrets of Super Achievers*

THINK OF ME

When you, by chance, may think of me

Remember, please, some kindness

That once or twice I may have shown

When I forgot the blindness

Of prejudice or hate and spite

And showed unselfish care,

And shared a day or dreamed a night

And left no hurting there.

And if some part of what is me

Some day you seek to take

And make it into what you'd be

I hope for each our sake

The part so easy to recall

So fast to come again

Will sing of spring and love for all

And leave no room for pain.

Joye Kanelakos
from *Discovering Joye*

Sometimes you find the strength within yourself simply because someone else believes you can do it.

Jim Stovall
from *You Don't Have To Be Blind To See*

More people fail to start than fail to succeed. There is no shame in striking out while offering your best efforts and being willing to get up to the plate again.

Jim Stovall
from *Ultimate Productivity*

If you make a decision and then find you've made the wrong choice — make a new decision!

Jim Stovall
from *You Don't Have To Be Blind To See*

Minutes, hours, and days are all you have to invest in making your future what you want it to be. Invest them wisely.

Jim Stovall
from *Wisdom for Winners*

Every life's journey is filled with problems. These problems have solutions that create greater opportunities and more problems.

Jim Stovall
from *The Ultimate Journey*

In order to have a good life, you have to have a series of good years. In order to have a good year, you must have a series of good months. In order to have a good month, you must have a series of good weeks. And, therefore, in order to have a good week, you must have a series of good days, beginning today.

Jim Stovall
from *Discovering Joye*

The people who watch the Narrative Television Network are emotional about NTN. It's not just an idea to them. It's not just a program format. It's hope. NTN opens a new door for them. It gives them a new means of enrichment for their lives. It sends a message to them that says, "Somebody in television cares about me."

Jim Stovall
from *You Don't Have To Be Blind To See*

One of the most amazing things I have discovered through the process of meeting many millionaires and becoming one myself is the fact that millionaires rarely focus on money. Millionaires have a tendency to focus on people, service, creativity, and producing value.

Jim Stovall
from *The Millionaire Map*

The basis of our American society is that we all are created *equal*. But it is difficult and not at all advisable to ignore the perception that some of us are more equal than others. To our good fortune, there is a rare benevolence common to our society that motivates us to iron out these inequalities.

William K. Coors
from *Success Secrets of Super Achievers*

Only by accepting full responsibility for your *past*, which has resulted in your *present*, can you then take control of your actions *today* and create a successful *tomorrow*.

Jim Stovall
from *Ultimate Productivity*

If you could have anything, what would you wish for?

Jim Stovall
from *The Lamp*

Remember that in every defeat there lies a seed of a greater victory. Go out and find that seed, and you will live a marvelous life.

Jim Stovall
from *Winners' Wisdom*

I believe love, honor, morals, and respect to all, including oneself, should be our top priorities.

John Agar
from *Success Secrets of Super Achievers*

There were two warring tribes in the Andes, one that lived in the lowlands and the other high in the mountains. The mountain people invaded the lowlanders one day, kidnapped a baby, and took the infant with them back up into the mountains. Although the lowlanders didn't know how to climb the mountain, they sent out their best party of fighting men to bring the baby home. After climbing only a few hundred feet after several days of effort, the lowlander men decided that the cause was lost, and they prepared to return to their village below.

As they were packing their gear for the descent, they saw the baby's mother — with the baby strapped to her back — coming down the mountain that they had been unable to climb. One man greeted her and said, "How did you climb this treacherous mountain when we, the strongest and most able men in the village, couldn't do it?"

She shrugged her shoulders and said, "It wasn't your baby."

Your goal, your dream, your sense of personal destiny,

is your baby. Nobody will care for it, rescue it, or work for it like you will. Don't expect it of others. Do expect that kind of care and hard work on your part. And, do expect that you will need to pursue your dream with that kind of single-minded focus.

Jim Stovall
from *You Don't Have To Be Blind To See*

It is better to do the right thing adequately than the wrong thing well.

Jim Stovall
from *Wisdom for Winners*

I have found that whether in the field of sports or in everyday life, one must possess many of the same qualities in order to achieve success. Some of these qualities would include dedication, hard work, honesty, integrity, leadership, loyalty, self-discipline, treating people fairly, teamwork, and having a positive attitude. Equally important to this foundation is a strong sense of duty to family and friends, and service to society.

Lamar Hunt
from *Success Secrets of Super Achievers*

A wise man once said, "Don't ask for advice from anyone who doesn't have what you want."

Jim Stovall
from *Success Secrets of Super Achievers*

I believe that for every goal in our lives, there is some step that can be taken today. It's important to have lifelong objectives and long term goals, but remember they don't mean anything unless we embrace the eternal truth that when you boil life down to its essence, *now* is the only thing that really matters.

Jim Stovall
from *Winners' Wisdom*

Problems should not be avoided but embraced and overcome. They give us an opportunity to grow bigger and help those around us.

Jim Stovall
from *Discovering Joye*

Just because you're moving, it doesn't mean you're moving in the right direction.

Jim Stovall
from *Ultimate Productivity*

Gratitude provides a balance between the things we have and those we want.

> Jim Stovall
> from *The Ultimate Life*

Our work is how we give ourselves to the world and leave a legacy behind.

> Jim Stovall
> from *The Gift of a Legacy*

Continue to excel at the things you do best, but focus your effort and energy on those things you want to do better.

> Jim Stovall
> from *Wisdom for Winners*

Giving money to other people and important causes not only improves them, but it will improve you.

> Jim Stovall
> from *The Millionaire Map*

Science and the quest for knowledge are not a destination but a lifelong, never-ending journey.

> Jim Stovall
> from *Wisdom of the Ages*

You will never outgrow your need for monitoring the quality of your life, your activities, and your possessions.

Jim Stovall
from *You Don't Have To Be Blind To See*

Unfortunately, we do not always get what we want or deserve or earn. We do, however, inevitably get what we expect. Life isn't so much what happens to us as it is how we perceive what happens to us.

Jim Stovall
from *Wisdom for Winners*

As a person who has struggled with reading problems all of my life, I believe that people who learn differently look at the world from unique perspectives. By identifying what gets in the way of learning for students, we are able to nurture their strengths, improve their self-esteem, and teach them the skills they will need to become our inventors, leaders, and entrepreneurs.

As parents, clinicians, and teachers, we have the opportunity—and the responsibility—to positively influence our children's lives.

Charles Schwab
from *Success Secrets of Super Achievers*

Think of all the people in your life who have left you a legacy of greatness. Many of these people were friends or loved ones who have passed away. The lessons they have taught you are their legacy to you. Your application of those lessons and your ultimate success is the only fitting memorial and tribute to them.

Jim Stovall
from *The Way I See the World*

If you will keep your personal definition of success in the forefront of your mind as you move into your future by pursuing your mission with passion, your tomorrows will be different from your today.

Jim Stovall
from *Ultimate Productivity*

Everybody has seed ideas. Recognize your ideas as seeds and cultivate them.

Jim Stovall
from *You Don't Have To Be Blind To See*

A person who doesn't *make* a choice is no better off than a person who doesn't *have* a choice.

Jim Stovall
from *Ultimate Productivity*

LAUGH A LITTLE

Laugh a little

When the world tries to get you down.

Love a little

Just spread a little love around

Look up a little

When everyone else is looking down.

Look up a little

And laugh in the middle with love.

Kelly Morrison,
from the album *Love and Dreams*, by Kelly Morrison

Never, never, never let somebody else define your success for you. Only you can determine what you want to be, do, and have.

Jim Stovall
from *You Don't Have To Be Blind To See*

You can earn money or lose it. You can build a building, tear it down, and build another, but today can never be replaced.

Jim Stovall
from *Wisdom for Winners*

Regardless of the legacy we receive, love is the legacy we should leave behind.

Jim Stovall
from *The Gift of a Legacy*

I'm a firm believer that no one with experience ever has to take a back seat to someone with a theory.

Jim Stovall
from *The Millionaire Map*

Success takes a lot of things, son. All working together. But I guess the place to start is that you can't be a sheep. You gotta be the bellwether. A leader, Red. You've got to learn how to be a leader of men to make things happen for yourself.

Peter Fonda
from *The Ultimate Life* movie

I am pleased that my career has brought laughter and entertainment to people, but I consider it a rare privilege that I have caused people from time to time to stop and think about who they are and how they stand on important issues in their lives and in the world.

Jack Lemmon
from *Success Secrets of Super Achievers*

Families give us our roots, our heritage, and our past. They also give us the springboard to our future.

Jim Stovall
from *The Ultimate Life*

Life's journey may last many years, but to reach our destination, we must travel well each day.

Jim Stovall
from *The Ultimate Journey*

Your dream must be *your* dream. If you are trying to fulfill another person's dream for your life, you'll always feel hindered in some way. And when a crisis comes — an adversity, a problem you can't readily solve, a point of termination — you will likely abandon the dream that isn't yours and feel a great sense of failure in the process. Make sure the dreams you are pursuing are ones that flow out of your desires.

Jim Stovall
from *You Don't Have To Be Blind To See*

The ultimate life is locked away inside each of us. Love is the key.

Jim Stovall
from *The Ultimate Life*

We can live out our wildest dreams and greatest imagined successes if we will simply suspend the disbelief that is keeping us anchored to our current mediocrity.

Jim Stovall
from *Wisdom for Winners*

Even though the World Wide Web allows us to do business in the blink of an eye with thousands of people around the world, the dynamic is as old as the first trade. You must provide value in the exchange within a comfortable and pleasant environment to do business. In order to prosper in the 21st century, we must do business using the latest technology — and the most ancient methods.

Jim Stovall
from *Winners' Wisdom*

Learn to work smarter, not harder; quicker, not more hurried; and productively, not just actively.

Jim Stovall
from *Ultimate Productivity*

Success is service to humanity.

Michael DeBakey, M.D.
from *Success Secrets of Super Achievers*

Priorities are the day-to-day mundane things that must be done. Possibilities are the big picture, long-range, creative pursuits that outline our potential greatness.

> Jim Stovall
> from *Wisdom for Winners*

No matter what situation or circumstance you are facing, you have the option of making decisions about your life. What appears to be the ending need not be. It can be the point of a new beginning.

> Jim Stovall
> from *You Don't Have To Be Blind To See*

Hidden paths,

obscured by fears,

grown over by habits of worry and negativity from doubt,

begin to appear and invite us.

These paths are our great opportunities.

Our destinies.

Our inheritance waiting for us.

This is our "good luck" we have sought forever.

> Joye Kanelakos
> from *Discovering Joye*

Some people are born into wonderful families. Others have to find or create them. Being a member of a family is a priceless membership that we pay nothing for but love.

Jim Stovall
from *The Ultimate Gift*

As I stand here today, I would do it all over again. I'd take every step. I'd make every journey. I'd fly every mile. I'd try to climb every mountain. I'd do it all over again. I wouldn't change a thing. I'd lay it upon me and upon you and upon everybody who will listen.

I'd tell everybody to listen to God's voice.

Oral Roberts
from *Success Secrets of Super Achievers*

You have chosen where you are today, but you will choose today where you will be tomorrow.

Jim Stovall
from *Wisdom for Winners*

If there is not something worth dying for, there cannot be anything worth living for.

Jim Stovall
from *Wisdom of the Ages*

We have a great life when we learn from our past, plan our future, and live each day in the present.

> Jim Stovall
> from *The Gift of a Legacy*

There is no magic. You see, you can have anything you want in life if you are only willing to first believe. When you lose hope, you believe that there is no way out other than to give up. Many people get their eyes off of what is true and embrace a lie. Then they begin to believe that lie. In time, this lie becomes their truth, and their whole life is built around it. My message is this — that you can have anything you want in life, even happiness and forgiveness, if you are willing to just believe.

> Louis Gossett Jr.
> from *The Lamp* movie

Just because you're talking and someone else is listening doesn't mean you are communicating. Communication is the process of successfully getting thoughts and ideas from your mind to someone else's.

> Jim Stovall
> from *Ultimate Productivity*

Success is achievable without public recognition, and the world has many unsung heroes. The teacher who inspires you to pursue your education to your ultimate ability; the parents who taught you the noblest human principles; the coach who shows you the importance of teamwork; the spiritual leader who instills in you spiritual values and faith; the relatives, friends, and neighbors with whom you develop a reciprocal relationship of respect and support; the most menial workers who perform their best.

Michael DeBakey, M.D.
from *Success Secrets of Super Achievers*

Our lives should be lived not avoiding problems but welcoming them as challenges that will strengthen us so that we can be victorious in the future.

James Garner
from *The Ultimate Gift* movie

The world tells us not to believe it until you see it. I know that you'll see it when you believe it. You can envision a bigger and more personally fulfilling destiny for your life. And what you begin to see, you can begin to have.

Dr. Denis Waitley
from *Success Secrets of Super Achievers*

If I had to identify one factor that could make any person succeed, it would be understanding the power and significance of every day.

> Jim Stovall
> from *Discovering Joye*

Once you're a millionaire, your focus must shift from getting rich to staying rich. You don't want to fumble on the proverbial goal line.

> Jim Stovall
> from *The Millionaire Map*

Your destiny will always lie in front of you, challenging you and pulling you forward and upward in your life.

> Jim Stovall
> from *You Don't Have To Be Blind To See*

Today we are inundated with talk about all of our rights. We hear about civil rights, equal rights, women's rights, minority rights, and many other worthwhile principles. But when you come right down to it, you and I only have one right in this world, and that is the right to choose. We can't always choose what happens to us, but we can always choose what we are going to do about it. Only when we accept the fact that we are where we are because of choices we've made in the past can we live every day of the rest of our lives in the certain knowledge that we can do anything we want to do if we simply make the right choices.

> Jim Stovall
> from *Winners' Wisdom*

Focus more on who you are than on what you do. Ultimately, that's where your value lies.

> Jim Stovall
> from *You Don't Have To Be Blind To See*

If you will focus on reaching your own goals by helping people around the world reach their goals, you cannot fail. Life is still a matter of helping yourself by meeting the needs of others.

> Jim Stovall
> from *Wisdom for Winners*

If there's change in doing nothing, it's likely to be for the worse.

> Jim Stovall
> from *You Don't Have To Be Blind To See*

We learned very early on, over thirty years ago, that doing what we love to do — sing and entertain — would be the thing that would make us happy. To be successful at it would make us ecstatic. We also learned very early that happiness must always be the goal, never money.

You must love what you want to do so much that you are willing to do it for nothing.

The Statler Brothers
from *Success Secrets of Super Achievers*

My father was a rough, tough little Irishman who loved to drink and fight and stir things up. Underneath was a man who loved his family with a passion. Pop was hard on the outside and soft on the inside.

Being a fighter, he only gave me one piece of advice. "Jim," he would say, "keep your right hand high and your rear end off the floor."

God helps me do that every day. It's simple, but sometimes simple is best. Trust in God, and keep your right hand high and your rear end off the floor.

Jimmie Rodgers
from *Success Secrets of Super Achievers*

People and things in this world are rarely as they first appear. We must be willing to dig down to the treasure beneath and then dig deeper still to reveal the masterpiece inside other people and ourselves.

Jim Stovall
from *Discovering Joye*

There is no substitute for being your BEST:

- **B**alanced as a person and in your relationship to others;
- **E**nthusiastic and intense in your quest for greatness;
- **S**ingle-minded and focused in your pursuit of your own personal destiny;
- **T**enacious in your commitment to your goals and dreams.

Jim Stovall
from *You Don't Have To Be Blind To See*

While working in a brokerage house, I chanced upon a book with the imposing title, *How to Become an Actor*. As I recall, the first paragraph of the book contained a line that said something like, "The secret of becoming a successful actor is ENTHUSIASM." This gave me both hope and purpose.

I may not have had technique or even talent at that

time, but, by heaven, if there was one thing I *did* have, it was ENTHUSIASM!

Robert Young
from *Success Secrets of Super Achievers*

Being "squared away" is a good thing to be.

Jimmy Carter
from *You Don't Have To Be Blind To See*

One of the greatest mistakes that is made by the majority of people who are trying to reach a goal is the mistake of trying to reach someone else's goal. You can never have the passion necessary to reach the summit of the mountain unless it's your mountain.

Jim Stovall
from *The Way I See the World*

You cannot become a leader because you declare yourself one or because you decide to be. You have to earn the title and the position of leader. Earning the right to be a leader first requires you to possess traits that others wish to emulate; but unless you can communicate and demonstrate those traits in a way that others can discern, you are not really a leader.

Jim Stovall
from *Ultimate Productivity*

If you're ever going to open your eyes to your future, open them today. And, if you're ever going to make a run for your destiny and your dreams, do it now.

> Jim Stovall
> from *You Don't Have To Be Blind To See*

The most talented, gifted, and well-committed people don't always succeed. Often, the least likely among us rises to the top.

> Jim Stovall
> from *Wisdom for Winners*

Life is not going to be easy. For every "up" there seems to be a "down," and so much of what we make of this brief time on earth depends on how we view life.

> Bob Losure
> from *Success Secrets of Super Achievers*

Make today the most productive day of your life. Set boundaries. Focus your activities. Make choices that are aimed at your goal. I suspect you'll like the way you feel at the end of the day.

> Jim Stovall
> from *You Don't Have To Be Blind To See*

Although there is absolutely nothing wrong with enjoying material possessions, it is important to draw a distinction between the possessions we have and those possessions that have us. It is not important to be a "human having." It is only important to arrive as a "human *being*." Focus on who you are, and allow what you *have* to become a result of your personal success.

Jim Stovall
from *Winners' Wisdom*

We find success when we help all the boats rise and elevate ourselves as we lift up those around us.

Jim Stovall
from *Wisdom for Winners*

Tenacity and work go together like hand and glove. Your degree of tenacity as you pursue your dream is your work ethic.

Jim Stovall
from *You Don't Have To Be Blind To See*

Trying to get rich quick on every venture is the best way I know to get poor and stay that way.

Jim Stovall
from *The Millionaire Map*

Problems that do not defeat us serve to define us.

Jim Stovall
from *Discovering Joye*

LEGACY

If I had a legacy
There's something I'd like for it to be.
I'd give every living soul
A piece of the gift you gave to me.
Shadows are far too hard to climb.
You taught me to step into the light.
If I could help someone like me
This would be my legacy.

If you had a legacy,
What would you like for it to be?
What will your loved ones say?
How will you help them find their way?
What are the gifts you'll leave behind?
What are the treasures they will find?
It's right inside your dreams,
And it's your legacy.

Music and lyrics by Kelly Morrison
from the motion picture *The Ultimate Life*

It doesn't benefit you to work today unless you have a future, but you have no future unless you handle priorities today.

These are a few rules for building wealth:

1.   Spend less than you earn.

2.   Avoid borrowing money.

3.   Live on a budget.

4.   Save and invest regularly

> Jim Stovall
> from *Wisdom for Winners*

In my work, most of the fun in getting there is the getting there. There are many rewards to drawing a nationally syndicated comic strip like *Broom-Hilda*. One nice one is that people send you money every month and you can eat food and have a house and shoes and sox. Another is that sometimes somebody says that they enjoy what you do. It's impossible not to smile when that happens.

I have trouble believing that any IRS agent or fish cleaner enjoys himself on the job. I have trouble believing that any cartoonist doesn't. Each and every day, if we're doing what we're supposed to, it's fun!

> Russell Myers
> from *Success Secrets of Super Achievers*

Once you capture the vision of your future that contains your personal definition of success, you'll never be the same again.

Jim Stovall
from *Ultimate Productivity*

The way to build a great life is simply to string together a series of great days.

Jim Stovall
from *Winners' Wisdom*

If we truly are a product of what we think about all day, the most valuable property we can ever own would be a positive, self-affirming thought.

Jim Stovall
from *Winners' Wisdom*

Reggie Jackson once told me, "Jim, somehow deep down inside me, I developed such a will to win that the times I felt the best were when I was up against the best pitcher that the opposing team had, and he threw his fastest pitch at me — one I could never have hit on my best day as a hitter — and he knocked me down into the dirt and I came up out of that dirt with a smile on my face and said to the other team's catcher,

'You'd better tell your man that if that's the best pitch he can throw, he's going to have a long day out there.' I felt like a champion in those times because I know that a champion never lets the other guy get to him."

Jim Stovall
from *You Don't Have To Be Blind To See*

If you don't control your budget, no matter how much you obtain, you will never be wealthy. You will just be among the big league spenders.

Jim Stovall
from *The Millionaire Map*

OUR LEGACIES

Every footprint that we take
Makes a change where we have passed.
Small things there beneath our heel
Are changing where the print was cast.

What then could any difference make
When ruthless paths our courses take?
Beneath our heel some things will bend
Without the strength to rise again.

Joye Kanelakos
from *The Gift of a Legacy* and *Discovering Joye*

George Burns once told me that if you love your job, you never have to work a day in your life.

> Jim Stovall
> from *Ultimate Productivity*

Money seldom brings contentment, but those who spend themselves in service to others will find true wealth and prosperity.

> Jim Stovall
> from *Wisdom of the Ages*

I don't pretend to tell people how to live their lives other than to do the right thing and work hard. Everything else should take care of itself.

> Dave Anderson
> from *Success Secrets of Super Achievers*

In order to climb to the mountaintop and live at the financial peak, you've got to crawl out of the valley of debt where you find yourself and avoid the constant annoying financial pitfalls that want to drag you back into that dark and depressing financial hole where you started.

> Jim Stovall
> from *The Millionaire Map*

You are the only customer that matters, so keep selling to yourself and stay sold on your destiny.

> Jim Stovall
> from *The Way I See the World*

Money is the fruit of our efforts and the fuel for our dreams.

> Jim Stovall
> from *The Ultimate Life*

Nothing is more powerful than making a beginning, making a decision, starting a course.

> Jim Stovall
> from *You Don't Have To Be Blind To See*

Failure and success cannot occupy the same space. Let go of one to begin enjoying the other.

> Jim Stovall
> from *Wisdom for Winners*

Integrity is doing the right thing, even if nobody is watching.

> Jim Stovall as quoted in *Reader's Digest*; June, 1999, from *You Don't Have To Be Blind To See*

The number one thing you and I are confronted with via advertising is debt. Debt has become a high-demand consumer item. It controls many people's budgets and a lot of people's lives.

> Jim Stovall
> from *Wisdom for Winners*

SELF-ESTEEM. The magic words. If you won't muster any for you, nobody else will.

> Shirley Jones
> from *Success Secrets of Super Achievers*

This life we are living right now is not a practice game. It is the Super Bowl and the World Series and the Olympics all rolled up into one. If you do not feel that way about your life and what you do, you need to do something different or get a new attitude about the things you do now.

> Jim Stovall
> from *Winners' Wisdom*

Visualization directly relates to turning your desires into something that can be pursued.

> Jim Stovall
> from *You Don't Have To Be Blind To See*

Without persistence, it is impossible to experience success.

> Joseph Barbera
> from *Success Secrets of Super Achievers*

Sometimes you don't have to blast your way to success; you simply need to endure the hard times.

> Jim Stovall
> from *You Don't Have To Be Blind To See*

Out of all the accomplishments that I have ever achieved in life, the most rewarding is my personal relationship with God.

If you truly want a miracle performed in your life, ask God to forgive you of your sins, and hand Him the reins.

> Darren Daulton
> from *Success Secrets of Super Achievers*

As you go through your day today, look for new things and experiences you would like to add to your life. Be willing to be vulnerable enough to be bad in the beginning so you can perform masterfully in the future.

> Jim Stovall
> from *Wisdom for Winners*

There is plenty of success to go around, because success is always determined individually.

Jim Stovall
from *You Don't Have To Be Blind To See*

I don't know what the *how* solutions will be for you to solve the problems you encounter as you pursue the *what* of your goal, but I do know this: You need to approach the problems with an attitude of "I don't have the answer right now, but I will have the answer!"

And then keep your inner ears and eyes open for what you might hear and see. Stay sensitive to the people who come your way and the knowledge they might have. Be open to suggestions and receptive to innovative, creative ideas. The *how* will eventually reveal itself.

Jim Stovall
from *You Don't Have To Be Blind To See*

Achieving success can be wonderful, but it is a lot more satisfying if you can make a worthwhile difference in someone's life on your way up.

Jack Lemmon
from *Success Secrets of Super Achievers*

It's like anything else. You start at the beginning, and you do one thing at a time until the goal is reached. And if I might add a piece of advice, never focus on the money. If you focus on the money, your priorities will always be wrong; however, if you focus on the people you're serving, the colleagues you are working with, and the task you are performing, the money will always take care of itself.

Steve Forbes
from *The Gift of a Legacy*

Many people live on a budget which is limited only by how much money they have or can borrow on a regular basis. These people choose to let money control them instead of them taking control of their money.

Jim Stovall
from *The Millionaire Map*

You weren't put on this earth to have a safety net under you and a glass ceiling over you. You were put on this earth to do something unique. You are to be the champion of the course in life that has been set before you. Discover that course, and then pursue it with intensity.

Jim Stovall
from *You Don't Have To Be Blind To See*

I always wanted to be a singer. I don't think I chose this dream. I think, rather, it chose me.

We all have a special calling in life, and in our own way, we all have a "song." We don't have to change the world, but I believe we are expected to use our uniqueness to make some difference, small though it may be.

Each life is a journey, so get the "map" out, and follow the right roads toward your own destiny.

> Donna Fargo
> from *Success Secrets of Super Achievers*

Who we are is a tribute to those who have left us a legacy. Who we help others become will be our legacy.

> Jim Stovall
> from *The Gift of a Legacy*

Facing the facts is hard, but it's vital. Every truly successful person has faced reality and continues to face it squarely. The opposite of facing reality is living in a state of denial. And you are denying yourself your future and your potential.

> Jim Stovall
> from *You Don't Have To Be Blind To See*

People and circumstances will invariably conspire to seemingly attempt to ruin your day. They cannot ruin your day, but they can ruin your attitude, and you can ruin your day.

>Jim Stovall
>from *Discovering Joye*

Work is a journey we undertake for others that makes us who we are.

>Jim Stovall
>from *The Ultimate Journey*

Good things from history can save us time as we move toward our goals in life. Bad things from history can help us to avoid the pitfalls. Lessons not learned from the past are certain to be learned in the future as history repeats itself.

>Jim Stovall
>from *Wisdom for Winners*

Gratitude is not a product of celebrating getting all the things we wanted. Gratitude is a product of recognizing that we wanted all the things we got.

>Jim Stovall
>from *Discovering Joye*

Listen, and listen fully. Too many people are afraid of silence. It is as if something has to be happening all the time. But with silence, there is a reflection on what was really said, what was really meant by the remarks, and, yes, perhaps some passage of thought between that person and ourselves.

The Amazing Kreskin
from *Success Secrets of Super Achievers*

I believe there are three key ingredients in the recipe for success. I call them the "Three A's."

The first "A" is "Atmosphere." We need an encouraging atmosphere to achieve our potential.

The second "A" is "Attitude." We must believe we can reach our goals, and we must be willing to look beyond obstacles to reach them.

The last "A" is "Action." Without action, the other two "A's" get us nowhere. We have to jump in and make our dream happen.

Richard M. DeVos
from *Success Secrets of Super Achievers*

Living on a budget is not about doing without. It's a matter of making choices.

Jim Stovall
from *The Millionaire Map*

Choose to be the best person you can be. Put your head on your pillow at night and say, "I was the best person I could be today, and that's enough."

>Jim Stovall
>from *You Don't Have To Be Blind To See*

BELIEFS

>give rise to VALUES

>>give rise to DESIRES

>>>give rise to EFFORT and ENERGY

>>>>give rise to ACCOMPLISHMENT.

>Jim Stovall
>from *You Don't Have To Be Blind To See*

As life goes on, you learn many more things that will open doors to you that raise further questions, creating more things you wish you knew.

>Jim Stovall
>from *The Gift of a Legacy*

In our personal and professional lives, we have the opportunity to reach out to hundreds of people every day with an encouraging word, an act of kindness, or by simply taking a few moments to truly listen and help. We, as professionals, have a responsibility to positively impact the lives of others not only with our products and services, but by our examples.

Look around you. Then reach out to someone, and make a difference in their lives — and yours.

Jim Stovall
from *Winners' Wisdom*

Your values determine your character, and they set a framework for the choices you make as well as a framework for evaluating your success.

Jim Stovall
from *You Don't Have To Be Blind To See*

Accountability isn't limited to what we do. It extends to who we are. It's intricately interwoven with what we hold as values.

Jim Stovall
from *You Don't Have To Be Blind To See*

If there were an eleventh commandment and I could choose what it would be, I'd choose, "Thou shalt not kid thyself."

Jim Stovall
from *You Don't Have To Be Blind To See*

It is better to be involved with people you can trust because of the bridge you have built instead of only trusting them because of the boundary you have created.

Jim Stovall
from *Wisdom for Winners*

The next time you have the choice between feeding your ego, feeding your body, or feeding your mind, try feeding your mind and you will find that it will result in a permanent change that will be manifested in every area of your life.

Jim Stovall
from *Winners' Wisdom*

I defy you to find a statue or a monument ever erected to anyone because they were realistic. All dreamers, all achievers, all great people kept their child-like faith in their own dream and their ability to carry it out, and these great people had an inordinate gift to disregard the world's cries for reality. I challenge you to go through a single day exploring every aspect, not from what is realistic, but instead from what is possible.

Jim Stovall
from *Winners' Wisdom*

Someone said, "You are as happy as you decide to be." I think it was Lincoln, or Woody Allen. I don't know.

There are many different ways to measure success. Ghandi only owned one sheet and he was a success. I know billionaires who are miserable and satiated and don't know a moment of happiness.

It all boils down to spirit and thinking. Everything happens in the mind.

Phyllis Diller
from *Success Secrets of Super Achievers*

For every lock, there is a key. Being optimistic about a solution doesn't mean that you are blind to the problem. It means that you have faith that every problem can be solved in some way, at some time, by somebody. Every time you face a change or a major turning point, a person will show up who will be a catalyst for you. Watch for that person. Welcome what he or she has to offer.

Jim Stovall
from *You Don't Have To Be Blind To See*

Giving is an act involving one person giving to another. Giving a legacy can touch the whole world.

Jim Stovall
from *The Gift of a Legacy*

Love is not a goal you reach as part of your life's journey, but something you give and receive all along the way.

> Jim Stovall
> from *The Ultimate Journey*

Keeping a sense of humor can keep you balanced.

> Jim Stovall
> from *You Don't Have To Be Blind To See*

Be sure to explore the entire smorgasbord that life has to offer. Too many people exist on a diet of bread and water when the entire world is their banquet table.

> Jim Stovall
> from *The Way I See The World*

Stay focused. Stay focused. Stay focused. Your dream will compel you to take action.

> Jim Stovall
> from *You Don't Have To Be Blind To See*

Anything worth your time and money as you pursue your wealth goals is worthy of checking out and verifying.

> Jim Stovall
> from *The Millionaire Map*

Man should be judged by the deeds done to help his fellow man.

> Ted Turner
> from *Success Secrets of Super Achievers*

Whether it's a TV show, a movie, a book, an album, a personal appearance, or an interview like this, I never forget there's a guy at home who is my audience, and I try to treat him as I would like to be treated. I have never considered myself a star, but instead, just the average guy's embodiment who works in show business.

I hope to give people the impression that if Steve Allen can do that, anyone can, because that is certainly the case.

> Steve Allen
> from *Success Secrets of Super Achievers*

A job enjoyed is the beginning of a job mastered.

> Jim Stovall
> from *Wisdom of the Ages*

It is impossible to experience fear, hate, or defeat when we are laughing.

> Jim Stovall
> from *The Ultimate Life*

Tenacity is endurance. It has no end.

> Jim Stovall
> from *You Don't Have To Be Blind To See*

When I went back to try college for the second start, I found it was just as tough the second time as it was the first time. Once you've had a failure and embraced it, as I had the year before, it's easier to opt for a failure the second time. The pressure is off somehow. You once failed, you bailed, and you survived, so it's easier to accept failure and bail again. Success breeds success, but failure also breeds failure.

> Jim Stovall
> from *You Don't Have To Be Blind To See*

A millionaire map or any map can be the most critical element of getting from where you are to where you want to be, but the best organized and most detailed map in the world is useless unless you know one thing. Before you can establish your destination or even your route to get there, you must know exactly where you are today. Most people not only have no money, they don't even know how far in debt they really are.

> Jim Stovall
> from *The Millionaire Map*

The first step into your future is likely to be the most difficult one. Take it anyway!

> Jim Stovall
> from *You Don't Have To Be Blind To See*

Expectation is believing you can and will achieve your goal.

> Jim Stovall
> from *You Don't Have To Be Blind To See*

Help is always near; as near as we are to our inner selves. There is a "buffer" surrounding us of joy, laughter, acceptance which will separate the important from the ridiculous. Pray in your possible desperation, then laugh with God.

> Joye Kanelakos
> from *Discovering Joye*

To be successful, you must just keep working; keep working wherever you are. I truly live for my work, and I'm fortunate to have a family that understands that. My husband understands it, my son understands it, and the dog understands it. Just live for it!

> Carol Channing
> from *Success Secrets of Super Achievers*

Nature revolves in a perfect cycle, teaching its own innate wisdom.

> Jim Stovall
> from *Wisdom of the Ages*

Success is getting up each and every day and embracing life to the fullest, eager for the opportunities and possibilities the day holds.

> Jim Stovall
> from *You Don't Have To Be Blind To See*

Any process worth going through will get tougher before it gets easier. That's what makes learning a gift. Even if pain is your teacher.

> James Garner
> from *The Ultimate Gift* movie

To get motivated and then look for something to which to apply that motivation is to put the cart in front of the horse. The dream comes first, and then if you aren't motivated, you probably need to get a new dream.

> Jim Stovall
> from *You Don't Have To Be Blind To See*

We human beings, in our own frailty, often believe we need to get outside of ourselves, and even outside of our community, in order to travel to a different land to find the things we seek. Only when we look inside can we begin to understand the ultimate gift which allows us to appreciate everything in the world we have been given, both inside and outside ourselves.

> Jim Stovall
> from *The Gift of a Legacy*

Happiness is the real sense of fulfillment that comes from hard work.

> Joseph Barbera
> from *Success Secrets of Super Achievers*

The more elements of the big picture you can communicate to your team, the better your chances of success.

> Jim Stovall
> from *Ultimate Productivity*

It's in our ability to visualize that we truly test our desires and form them into dreams.

> Jim Stovall
> from *You Don't Have To Be Blind To See*

Real success requires respect for and faithfulness to the highest human values: honesty, integrity, self-discipline, dignity, compassion, humility, courage, personal responsibility, courtesy, and human service.

Michael DeBakey, M.D.
from *Success Secrets of Super Achievers*

My grandmother, who was blind, taught me some of the greatest lessons in living that I could ever learn. I came to realize what a great woman she was and how courageously she had met and overcome a tremendous challenge. She made the world better because she was in it, and she made me want to leave the world a better place than when I came into it — just like she had.

Janet Leigh
from *Success Secrets of Super Achievers*

CHANGE. There's always someone to tell you you have to. *Wrong. Don't.* Rather, spend time finding out who you *really are*. Work on being more of *that*. A lot better than the futile "gotta change" treadmill, which never really ends.

Shirley Jones
from *Success Secrets of Super Achievers*

You are only one quality decision away from a new beginning.

> Jim Stovall
> from *You Don't Have To Be Blind To See*

Every season is a gift, every day is an opportunity, and every moment is a treasure. Spend them all wisely.

> Jim Stovall
> from *Discovering Joye*

Nothing on this planet is more powerful than a person who has made a decision to achieve something.

> Jim Stovall
> from *You Don't Have To Be Blind To See*

You don't have a right to be anything less than your absolute best. Not only for your sake, but for those who will come after you.

> Jim Stovall
> from *You Don't Have To Be Blind To See*

Find out what the people need who are in the path of your destiny, and do your best to meet their needs.

> Jim Stovall
> from *You Don't Have To Be Blind To See*

You will hear your heartbeat when your life is in rhythm, and there is no doubt that you're doing what you were made to do. That's your heartbeat. That's when you're truly alive and not just existing. I want you to get your heartbeat back. You can if you are willing to believe you can.

> Louis Gossett Jr.
> from *The Lamp* movie

No one can be considered a failure who has a friend, and no one can be considered a success without one.

> Jim Stovall
> from *The Ultimate Life*

Learning is never done. Each peak of wisdom and knowledge reveals great vistas of possibility in the distance. As truth is revealed, it exposes more questions waiting to be answered.

> Jim Stovall
> from *Discovering Joye*

Become a student of your assets. Know what they are, and then work to develop them.

> Jim Stovall
> from *You Don't Have To Be Blind To See*

Examine your expectations, and you will find that somewhere along the way you came to expect the life you are experiencing at this moment.

> Jim Stovall
> from *Ultimate Productivity*

You can't give away credit fast enough. It always comes back to you.

> Jim Stovall
> from *You Don't Have To Be Blind To See*

Being grateful today makes you appreciate yesterday and anticipate tomorrow.

> Jim Stovall
> from *Discovering Joye*

We have faith in the eternal values, in being good, not being bad.

> Stan and Jan Berenstain
> from *Success Secrets of Super Achievers*

In most cases, successful people consider their failures to be important lessons that prepared them for success.

> Jim Stovall
> from *You Don't Have To Be Blind To See*

You can be assured that if a one-eyed, skinny kid with no special training or talent and no inside or outside help can make it by just trying and trying and trying, and taking chances...so can you!

> Jack Elam
> from *Success Secrets of Super Achievers*

For too many people, perfection becomes an unachievable ideal that creates an environment in which they simply never begin.

> Jim Stovall
> from *Ultimate Productivity*

Face up to the reality of what you can do, and you'll discover that there are, indeed, very few things you can't do.

> Jim Stovall
> from *You Don't Have To Be Blind To See*

Do what you love to do the most, whether you get paid for it or not. The result will be that, eventually, you will become very successful just doing what you love to do.

> Ray Conniff
> from *Success Secrets of Super Achievers*

The successful person leaves behind their values in addition to their valuables and a piece of themselves.

Jim Stovall
from *The Gift of a Legacy*

People who live in success come to expect success.

Jim Stovall
from *You Don't Have To Be Blind To See*

Don't wait for some magic moment to begin your pursuit of your goals and dreams. No matter what your goal or dream, you can start doing something today. Get with it!

Jim Stovall
from *You Don't Have To Be Blind To See*

If there's one thing I have learned, it is that I don't believe in complaining. You simply do the best you can with what you've got, and somehow it works out.

Fay Wray
from *Success Secrets of Super Achievers*

Focus on the goal, not the means. Consider money a tool—not an end in itself.

Jim Stovall
from *You Don't Have To Be Blind To See*

Life is the greatest teacher and the ultimate purveyor of wisdom.

Jim Stovall
from *Wisdom of the Ages*

We don't fail because we don't know what to do. We fail because we don't do what we know. Sigmund Freud tells us that insanity is defined as doing the same thing over and over, but continually expecting a different result. If you want a different result in your life, take a different action. Starting now.

Jim Stovall
from *Winners' Wisdom*

Ultimately, your destiny is *your* destiny. It's your purpose for living.

Jim Stovall
from *You Don't Have To Be Blind To See*

In this life, there is nothing more powerful than a person who has seen the path to destiny within their soul and is willing to pursue it.

Jim Stovall
from *The Ultimate Life*

I do not take credit for my own success. I put the whole process into God's hands. Trust Him and let Him show us the way. I gather strength from knowing that He will always be there for me, no matter what.

What God does not protect you from, He provides you through.

Jimmie Rodgers
from *Success Secrets of Super Achievers*

Success is not a matter of "arriving," but of scaling one mountain and using it as a jumping-off point for the next peak.

Jim Stovall
from *Success Secrets of Super Achievers*

To achieve success, one must have a reasonable, commendable, and achievable goal and must pursue it with determination and dedication. If the goal is humanitarian, the joy will be all the greater.

Michael DeBakey, M.D.
from *Success Secrets of Super Achievers*

Even little lies can immobilize.

Jim Stovall
from *You Don't Have To Be Blind To See*

Our dreams launch us on every one of life's journeys, and they are there to meet us at the end.

> Jim Stovall
> from *The Ultimate Journey*

If you are not happy now, there is no specific thing that you are going to purchase that will make you happy. Don't confuse "having" with "being."

> Jim Stovall
> from *Wisdom for Winners*

I consider every person I meet is my superior in that I can learn something from him or her that I don't already know.

> Jim Stovall
> from *You Don't Have To Be Blind To See*

Most Americans fail to reach their financial goals, not because they don't have enough money. They fail because they don't play great defense and control the money they have.

> Jim Stovall
> from *The Millionaire Map*

Never make any decision before you have to.

> Jim Stovall
> from *The Ultimate Life*

Some friendships are a legacy left to us by those who have gone before. Other friendships are legacies we will leave behind.

> Jim Stovall
> from *The Gift of a Legacy*

The journey of life is a matter of traveling well rather than reaching a destination.

> Jim Stovall
> from *The Ultimate Journey*

Productivity is related to what you accomplish, not what you do.

> Jim Stovall
> from *You Don't Have To Be Blind To See*

To fully enjoy life, one must know how to enjoy the inevitable rainy days.

> William K. Coors
> from *Success Secrets of Super Achievers*

Don't make the mistake of prioritizing your schedules instead of scheduling your priorities. Remember that yesterday is history, tomorrow is a mystery, and today is a gift. That's why it's called "the present." Be sure to live it that way and plan to live it that way in the future.

> Jim Stovall
> from *Winners' Wisdom*

As a blind person, I realize that running into posts is part of the price I pay for getting out of my little room at home where I had intended to spend the rest of my life. I could still be sitting there. But I'm willing to fall or run into something or injure myself in some way to have the freedom of getting out of my room and into the mainstream of life.

You may injure yourself as you pursue your goal — dent your reputation, suffer a bruise to your ego, get a black eye for a mistake you make. But don't let it stop you. Don't let it send you back to a place of fears, doubts, and discouragement.

Refuse to give up.

Keep moving forward.

You'll get there!

> Jim Stovall
> from *You Don't Have To Be Blind To See*

A people must know their past before they can understand their present and move into their future.

Jim Stovall
from *Wisdom of the Ages*

We become rich in this life when we calculate our wealth, not based on the money we have but, instead, the friendships we hold.

Jim Stovall
from *Discovering Joye*

Success lies in the balance between seeking and striving on one hand and being peaceful and content on the other.

Jim Stovall
from *Wisdom for Winners*

I have heard it said that you have to "pay the price for success." I don't necessarily believe in that. I believe when you follow your passion, you will enjoy the price of success. If you don't follow your passion, you will pay the price for failure.

Jim Stovall
from *Winners' Wisdom*

It's a whole lot more important to know what to look at
than how well you see it.

George Washington Stovall
from *You Don't Have To Be Blind To See*

CORNERSTONES

If I am to dream, let me dream magnificently.

Let me dream grand and lofty thoughts and ideals

That are worthy of me and my best efforts.

If I am to strive, let me strive mightily.

Let me spend myself and my very being

In a quest for that magnificent dream.

And, if I am to stumble, let me stumble but persevere.

Let me learn, grow,

And expand myself to join the battle renewed

Another day and another day and another day.

If I am to win, as I must,

Let me do so with honor, humility, and gratitude

For those people and things that have made winning possible

And so very sweet.

For each of us has been given life as an empty plot of ground

With four cornerstones.

These four cornerstones are the ability to dream,

The ability to strive,

The ability to stumble but persevere,

And the ability to win.

The common man sees his plot of ground as little more

Than a place to sit and ponder the things that will never be.

But the uncommon man sees his plot of ground as a castle,

A cathedral,

A place of learning and healing.

For the uncommon man understands

That in these four cornerstones

The Almighty has given us anything – and everything.

Jim Stovall
from *Winners' Wisdom*

Believing in my own success is a constant battle. It is the ultimate battle that we all face, which is the battle for the mind. It is the only real battle in the world. I want you to know that, as you undertake your battle for belief, *I already believe in you.*

Jim Stovall
from *Success Secrets of Super Achievers*

Money can help us along our journey and buy us a vehicle for the trip, but it is never a destination.

Jim Stovall
from *The Ultimate Journey*

If you don't enjoy the journey, there is no destination worth the effort.

Jim Stovall
from *Wisdom for Winners*

The person who is the best judge of your competency isn't a teacher, a consumer, or a friend — it's you.

Jim Stovall
from *You Don't Have To Be Blind To See*

Your personal success goal had better be fully in line with your deepest passion.

Jim Stovall
from *Ultimate Productivity*

There's no substitute for homework. It's critical to every successful venture.

Jim Stovall
from *You Don't Have To Be Blind To See*

You can be a success by having a positive effect on the lives of others. If what you are doing with your life is hurting the ones you love, you will never be able to define yourself as a success.

> Pat Boone
> from *Success Secrets of Super Achievers*

Folks, I remember when we couldn't laugh about our differences as people, and it was a terrible world. Now we are getting to the point that we can laugh about the fact that we are different, and in that, I see hope for a better tomorrow.

> Don Rickles
> from *You Don't Have To Be Blind To See*

We should devote our most serious efforts to bringing about mental peace. I have found that the greatest degree of inner tranquility comes from the development of love and compassion.

> His Holiness, the Dalai Lama
> from *Success Secrets of Super Achievers*

The Search for Wisdom: Wisdom will benefit all people and will forever improve the lives of all humanity.

> Jim Stovall
> from *Wisdom of the Ages*

Dreams are the essence of all we can become.

Jim Stovall
from *The Ultimate Life*

Enjoy things that are valuable, but treasure the things that really matter. It doesn't matter how gifted, talented, or well-educated you might be. You will succeed or fail as a part of a team, and you will find happiness and contentment as a part of a family, a community, and a society.

Jim Stovall
from *Wisdom for Winners*

To know that one is a good person, thoughtful to others, and not petty, makes one a great success.

Jacqueline Bisset
from *Success Secrets of Super Achievers*

If I could pass one piece of election reform legislation, I would make it a law that it would be a crime for anyone to complain about the government or any elected official if the person complaining did not vote. Get involved in the system.

Jim Stovall
from *Wisdom for Winners*

Laughter is good medicine for the soul. Our world is desperately in need of more medicine.

Jim Stovall
from *The Ultimate Gift*

Success comes when you live a life of productivity on a mission toward a worthwhile goal.

Jim Stovall
from *Ultimate Productivity*

A beautiful face gets you the first five minutes. After that, you're on your own.

Loretta Young
from *Success Secrets of Super Achievers*

I believe in the old adage: Failure is not final. Failure is fertilizer.

Jim Stovall
from *The Millionaire Map*

Your capacities to think and feel are your two greatest assets. They propel you forward. Walk boldly into your tomorrow!

Jim Stovall
from *You Don't Have To Be Blind To See*

Knowledge is the key to anything you want in this life. I have often heard it said by one of the great leaders in the field of personal development, my friend Charlie "Tremendous" Jones, that, "You will be the same person five years from today except for the people you meet and the books you read." Virtually anything that you want to know is available for you within a few short miles of where you live — at the public library. As one of the great cheerleaders of the written word always said, "The more books you read, the taller you grow."

Jim Stovall
from *Winners' Wisdom*

Your dream for your life must have a dream element to it. It must be something that calls for you to extend yourself, to push yourself — and in that, to grow or change or develop.

Jim Stovall
from *You Don't Have To Be Blind To See*

Becoming a millionaire is fairly simple, but it's not easy.

Jim Stovall
from *The Millionaire Map*

I awoke this morning

With a prayer of gratefulness,

A prayer of hopefulness and joy.

To a God of love,

I asked for love –

A house full of it.

I seek and expect a home

Bursting its seams

And raising the roof with love,

Driving out everything else

And making a place for angels to enter

And sing of the promise,

"Where love is, there I am, also."

Joye Kanelakos
from *Discovering Joye*

If you knew that you were going to take on the characteristics of the people with whom you spend the most time, would you consider adding some more positive influences to your daily dose of friends and associates?

Jim Stovall
from *Wisdom for Winners*

People who do not exercise their right to choose will live with the choices that others make for them.

Jim Stovall
from *The Way I See The World*

There are many blessings which are available to those with the will and imagination — and the guts — to seek them out, polish them, and then use them as they are intended to be used.

Douglas Fairbanks, Jr.
from *Success Secrets of Super Achievers*

All of us have handicaps of one sort or another, and it is important that we lend a hand to each other so we can share the gifts we have been given.

Ted Turner
from *Success Secrets of Super Achievers*

If you don't love what you do, you will be competing against people who do love their business. They will outperform you every time because their business is like their baby.

Jim Stovall
from *The Millionaire Map*

In the final analysis, the only failure is to stop trying.

Jim Stovall
from *The Way I See The World*

Every legacy starts with a great life, and every great life starts with a great plan.

Jim Stovall
from *The Gift of a Legacy*

By 1964, Marty Ingels had become a successful actor and comedian, but one night his life came crashing down on — of all places — *The Tonight Show*. There, in front of millions of people, he had an anxiety attack. Some members of the backstage crew drove him home and left him on the floor in front of his television set. For the next nine months, three weeks, and four days, Marty Ingels lay on that very spot in that dingy apartment building. Had it not been for a neighbor, he said, who brought him hot food, he would have died.

To this day, no one knows what brought him down, but one Sunday afternoon, it suddenly left.

Marty says of the experience, "I came back again, older, wiser, stronger for what I'd survived and determined to keep the list of fervent promises I had made to myself while I was down there, bent and beaten. Those promises spoke of not making any of the mistakes I'd made before, of having the strength to hold tight to the dream, no matter what, and most of all, of never being scared again."

Marty Ingels
from *Success Secrets of Super Achievers*

HOLD ON TO YOUR DREAMS

Hold on to your dreams
And stand tall,
Even when those around you
Would force you to crawl.

Hold on to your dreams
As a race you must run,
Even when reality whispers
You will never be done.

Hold on to your dreams
And wait for the miracle to come,
Because on that miraculous day,
Your dreams and your reality
Will merge into one.

Jim Stovall
as published by The National Library of Poetry

There is a master plan for each of us that includes a grand design for all the days of our lives.

Jim Stovall
from *Discovering Joye*

There is no such thing as an insignificant person. Each life has value.

There is no such thing as an insignificant relationship. All of them are important.

There's no such thing as an insignificant day. All are precious.

And when we are living our lives the way we are supposed to live, there's no such thing as an insignificant moment, because each moment holds within it the seed of our ability to change our lives by changing our minds.

Jim Stovall
from *You Don't Have To Be Blind To See*

Only when we accept the fact that we are where we are because of choices we've made in the past can we live every day of the rest of our lives in the certain knowledge that we can do anything we want to do if we simply make the right choices. Your destiny awaits.

Jim Stovall
from *Wisdom for Winners*

Nothing is more powerful than a

person

who knows his or her destiny

and has chosen

now

as the time to pursue it.

Today's the day!

Jim Stovall
from *You Don't Have To Be Blind To See*

Quotes and poems used throughout this book are taken from these exceptional products by Jim Stovall:

What would you do to inherit a million dollars? Would you be willing to change your life? Jason Stevens is about to find out in Jim Stovall's *The Ultimate Gift*. *The Ultimate Gift* is also available as a DVD movie

Fiction, Hardcover, 156 pages

In *You Don't Have to Be Blind to See*, Jim Stovall shows you how to choose a new path that leads to success in every area of your life. This powerful, inspiring book will help you dream big dreams and define success for yourself. It will also give you the tools to make your dreams come true and succeed on your own terms.

Nonfiction, Hardcover, 278 pages

Winners' Wisdom is a weekly, syndicated success column written by Jim Stovall. It is carried in magazines, newspapers and world-wide online publications.

WINNERS' WISDOM

To order, please visit www.JimStovall.com.

Once upon a time, in a land far away, an enchanted kingdom was ruled by a much-loved king who, through his uncommon wisdom and insight, led his people through many difficult times to a period of peace, prosperity and happiness such as the kingdom had never known. Nearing the end of his reign, the king contemplates his legacy. What would be a fitting memorial to his time on the throne?

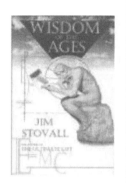

Fiction, Hardcover, 123 pages

Want to know the best way to reach a mountain top? Ask a person who's been there! That's the approach Jim Stovall has taken in *Success Secrets of Super Achievers*. Jim Stovall interviewed dozens of top-level people — people widely known and admired in business, politics religion, and entertainment — asking them 2 compelling questions: How do you define success, and what does it take to be happy?

Nonfiction, 190 pages

Uncovering the treasures inside ordinary people, places, things and ourselves, *Discovering Joye* is where art meets science and results in success in every facet of life. Based on the work of Joye Kanelakos, an unknown poet who revealed her extensive poetic work to her children on her deathbed.

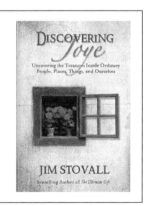

Nonfiction, 176 pages

To order, please visit www.JimStovall.com.

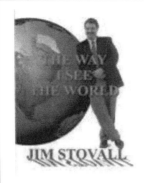

The Way I See the World by Jim Stovall goes beyond theory and rhetoric. Stovall uses his own life experience of overcoming the challenges of blindness to achieve great success. Through his own struggles, you will see your own possibilities and your ultimate destiny.

Nonfiction, Paperback, 112 pages

"*Millionaire Map* is the book I wished was available 30 years ago when I was desperate and broke with only a dream of one day being a millionaire. Now, as a multimillionaire, I want to share the wisdom I've gained from the journey and provide other travelers with a map to guide them on their journey." – Jim Stovall

Nonfiction, 160 pages

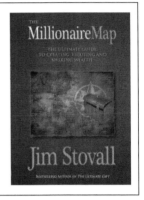

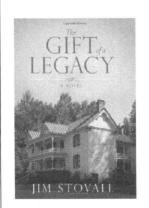

Jim Stovall continues his best-selling Ultimate Gift series with *The Gift of a Legacy*. Joey Anderson's great-grandmother touched many lives during her lifetime. Joey, however, has little interest in his great-grandmother's final wishes — until he learns that she's left him Anderson House, her successful bed-and-breakfast. The inheritance has a catch: he must live at Anderson House and follow strict instructions. Can Joey meet her challenge?

Fiction, 208 pages

To order, please visit www.JimStovall.com.

The Lamp, a movie based on Jim Stovall's novel, stars Academy Award winner Louis Gossett, Jr. A grieving man gets a second chance to really live when a mysterious stranger gives him a message: "What I am about to tell you will change your life. You can have anything you want, including true happiness, and I am going to tell you the secret of how to get it."

DVD

When his wealthy grandfather dies, trust fund baby Jason Stevens inherits his grandfather's crash course on life: 12 tasks (gifts) designed to challenge Jason. It sends him on a journey of self-discovery, forcing him to reevaluate his priorities and determine what he thinks the most important things in life really are. Starring: James Garner

DVD

To order, please visit www.JimStovall.com.

Poems, Quotes, and Things to Think About
is proudly published by:

Creative Force Press
Guiding Aspiring Authors to Release Their Dream

www.CreativeForcePress.com

Do You Have a Book in You?

16286374R00087

Made in the USA
San Bernardino, CA
27 October 2014